501
GOLF JOKES
for (Almost) All Occasions

FROM THE FIRST TEE TO THE 18TH GREEN—
AND EVERYTHING IN BETWEEN

COMPILED AND EDITED BY
FRANKLIN DOHANYOS

ILLUSTRATIONS BY JOHN HARROW

CITADEL PRESS
Kensington Publishing Corp.
www.kensingtonbooks.com

CITADEL PRESS books are published by

Kensington Publishing Corp.
850 Third Avenue
New York, NY 10022

All Kensington titles, imprints, and distributed lines are available at special quantity discounts for bulk purchases for sales promotions, premiums, fund raising, educational, or institutional use. Special book excerpts or customized printings can also be created to fit specific needs. For details, write or phone the office of the Kensington special sales manager: Kensington Publishing Corp., 850 Third Avenue, New York, NY 10022, attn: Special Sales Department, phone 1-800-221-2647.

Citadel Press logo Reg. U.S. Patent and Trademark Office
Citadel Press is a trademark of Kensington Publishing Corp.

First printing: February, 2001

10 9 8 7 6 5 4 3 2 1

Printed in the United States of America

Cataloging Data can be obtained from the Library of Congress

ISBN 0-8065-2155-4

This is to all the golfers out there, from novice to pro, and to Larry, whose many tips on how to tee off for the first time had me twisted like a pretzel. *Thanks for not laughing too hard! See you at Keweenaw.*

ACKNOWLEDGMENTS

I would like to thank all the family, friends, clients, acquaintances, and strangers who took the time to pass along a funny golf joke or two. I enjoyed hearing and reading them all.

CONTENTS

INTRODUCTION

Perhaps the biggest and funniest joke related to this book is my own golf score. I don't want to say I'm a bad golfer, but when clients ask me what my handicap is, I tell them I own clubs—that's my handicap! When I golf, emergency sirens go off in three counties and local wildlife heads for higher ground. I'm hired to play at corporate golf outings so the bad golfers in the company look good. The rangers at all the courses in Michigan commonly refer to me as their favorite Shemp!

Maybe it's the fact that at nine years old I walked into the swing of a neighborhood friend's practice tee shot and received nine stitches above my left eyebrow, or maybe it's because every time I golf I need to take out a small loan to pay for lost golf balls. Either way, my golfing stinks! If it weren't for the cigars, I don't know if I'd play at all.

Despite my lousy golf game and the fact that I've hit various objects and animals with my tee shots (I think the DNR is still looking for me!), I enjoy it. Golfing makes me laugh! So this is my book of favorite golf jokes. It's a salute to the hearty duffer who's out on the links at six o'clock on a warm Sunday morning, the one who's crazy enough to play in freezing November snow flurries, and the one who's brave enough to bring his wife even though her handicap is lower than his. And remember, if you're ever out on the course on a bright sunny day when you suddenly hear warning sirens and see people taking cover, don't fret. It's probably just me teeing up on the next hole. *Enjoy!*

—FD

501 GOLF JOKES
for (Almost) All Occasions

BAD GOLFERS

1. A golfer was trying everything to beat his personal best at his favorite course, but kept tearing up sod with his tee shots and fairway shots. Near the end of a round he turned to his caddie and said, "Man, I'd move heaven and earth to break a hundred on this course."

   The caddie said, "Try heaven. You've already moved most of the earth."

   • • •

2. All the caddies at the local country club hated Barney, one of the club's longstanding members, because he was a hack golfer, always blamed the caddies for his poor game, and was the cheapest man on earth. When he pulled into the lot, all the caddies would hide or pretend to be busy helping other golfers. Well, one day Barney pulled into the lot and the caddies scattered, all except for one who happened to be in the rest room at the time. When the unsuspecting caddie came out of the rest room, there was Barney waiting for him. Barney and the caddie left for the first tee. By the seventh hole Barney was twenty-one strokes over par, on course for another banner day. He hit his tee shot on eight into some nearby trees. The shot bounced off the trees like a pinball and came flying back at the caddie, nearly removing one of his family jewels and doubling him over. The caddie was in agony and furious.

When Barney asked what club he might use to help his driving, the caddie shouted, "Why don't you use your penis! You're going to screw it up anyway!"

• • •

3. A rich Texas oil man purchased a posh country club known for its beautiful course. One day he closed the course to the public and invited all the local media to come see it and play a round. One local TV sportscaster asked the man how each hole's par was determined. The man smiled and said, "Well, that's simple, son. Ya see, I own this course so it can be any par I want. Take that hole over there, for instance. That hole is a par-47, and yesterday I almost birdied the sucker."

• • •

4. Two singles arrived at the local country club for a round of golf and were paired up by the club pro. After a few minutes of discussion they learned that they both served in the armed forces in World War II. One was a former marine drill sergeant, and the other was an air force commander.

It wasn't long before they were talking about the war. They shared boot camp stories, war memories, and jokes about today's recruits. Everything was fine until the fourth hole, when the marine sergeant was finishing a story about how the marines were called in to stop a runaway tank. "Of course, you know, the marines are the bravest men in the armed forces."

The commander dropped his five iron and looked at him. "Just what the heck do you mean by that?"

The sergeant replied, "Who do you call in to take new territory? Who do you call in when you're outnumbered? Who gets chosen for the most covert operations?"

The commander replied, "Really? Well, while you are hiding in the bushes, who is in the sky, visible to the enemy? Who do *you* call for backup when you're outnumbered? And who is always called in during a losing battle? There's no question. The air force has the bravest men." The two men debated the subject throughout the entire round, each providing good examples to prove his point. After finishing, they decided to have a beer at the clubhouse and continue debating.

After about an hour, the marine sergeant stood up and said, "Well, my wife is fixing a big dinner for some old war buddies and their wives. I need to get back home. How about we play again next week?"

The air force commander put down his bottle and shook the sergeant's hand and said, "I owe you an apology. Anyone who played like you did today and is willing to come back to the same golf course is a much braver man than myself!"

• • •

5. A golf club was having a competition in which a new car was being given away to anyone who hit a hole in one on the eighteenth hole, a long par-3. The car was on display about forty yards from the hole. No one had any luck winning the car when the final foursome was ready to tee off on the eighteenth. The first three members in the group didn't come close. The fourth member, a real hack golfer, grabbed a 5-iron and teed his ball. He took a mighty swing, sending the ball directly toward the car and through the windshield. A stunned silence fell over the crowd.

Suddenly the club pro came running over to the hack golfer, "Hey, moron, when we say hole in one, we mean put the ball in the cup, not the car!"

• • •

6. A foursome of hack golfers walked into the clubhouse for a few beers after a round of golf. The bartender took their drink orders and asked how their game went. The first guy said he had a good round, with thirty-two rides. The second guy said he did all right, with nineteen rides. The third guy said not too bad since he had twelve rides. The fourth guy was disappointed and said that he played badly—only two rides. The bartender didn't want to seem stupid so he just smiled and walked away. He called over to the pro shop and asked the pro what the heck these guys meant when they said rides.

The pro laughed and said, "A ride is when you hit a shot long enough to take a ride on the golf cart."

• • •

7. A guy comes home from the golf course and says, "I'm not playing golf with Bill anymore."

His wife says, "Why not?"

"Tell me, would you play with a guy who slices every drive into other fairways, doesn't yell 'fore' when he's shooting near other people, rips up more sod than a bulldozer, loses more balls than he brings, drinks too much, and tells lousy jokes?" he asks.

"Of course not," she says.

"Well, neither will Bill!"

• • •

8. Two mathematicians go golfing one morning. Neither of them is very good at the game. After the first nine holes they decide to check their scores. One looks at the other one's score sheet and says, "How the hell did you get through grad school without being able to count past four!"

• • •

9. One golfer commenting on another's lucky shot: "Jimmy, for most people that would be considered a good shot. Considering you hit it, though, it's a brilliant shot!"

• • •

10. Before starting play, a hack golfer was bragging in the locker room to the club pro about his new set of graphite shaft clubs. After his round the hack went to the clubhouse for a few drinks. The club pro happened by and asked him how his new clubs worked out.

"Oh, great," said the hack, "they put twenty yards on my slice and left bigger divots."

• • •

11. A hack golfer, despised by the club pro and all the caddies, showed up for his usual Saturday round of slicing and divots. By the fifth hole the caddie was completely frus-

trated and by the sixteenth was ready to strangle the guy. After needing fifteen strokes on the seventeenth hole the hack said, "Caddie, I lost track. What should I take for this one?"

The irate caddie replied, "Beats me. Seems like a toss-up between cyanide and arsenic."

• • •

12. A hack golfer was determined to improve his game to impress his boss. He was on the links for eighteen holes after work one day. At the first hole he took a nine, blowing an easy six-foot putt. At the second hole he took a twelve, landing in three hazards. This continued at the third hole. By the fourth hole the guy blew a gasket and after every blown shot started tossing his clubs into water hazards or breaking them over his knee and on nearby trees. By the ninth hole he had destroyed or lost every club and didn't quite know what to do. He turned to his caddie and asked, "What the heck do I do now?"

A little upset with the guy, the caddie said, "I don't think the club has a rule that covers this, but will you be needing that sweater?"

• • •

13. A hack golfer recently purchased a new set of top-name clubs from the pro shop at his country club, thinking it would drastically improve his golf game. About a week later he stormed into the pro shop, threw the set of clubs on the counter, and demanded his money back. The pro shop manager heard the commotion and came out of his office to talk to the guy. "What seems to be the problem, sir?"

"Problem?! I'll tell you what the problem is," the guy snapped. "I bought these clubs to improve my game, and they don't work. The woods slice everything, the long irons continually put me in the rough, I get no backspin from the short irons, and this damn putter couldn't make a putt if I dug a channel straight to the cup!"

• • •

14. A young caddie was subpoenaed to testify in a case involving an accident he had witnessed. Oddly enough, the sitting judge happened to be the same poor golfer for whom he had caddied week after week at the country club. As the caddie was called up and approached the bench, the judge said, "Young man, have you ever taken an oath?"

"I'm not sure I know what you mean, Your Honor," said the caddie.

"An oath. You know, as in to tell the truth. Have you ever taken an oath?" asked the judge.

"I still don't get it," said the caddie.

"Do you know how to swear?" the judge snapped impatiently.

"Oh, swearing! Sure I do. I learn something new from you every week!"

• • •

15. An executive was invited to play a round of golf with his boss at the local country club. Wanting to make a good impression, he went to the golf store and purchased an entire new outfit, new shoes, and a new bag. He was preparing to leave when his wife stopped to compliment his new attire.

"Wow, look at you," she said. "New sweater vest, new shirt, new knickers, new shoes, and new bag. You look great. Too bad you have to spoil it all by playing golf!"

• • •

16. A hack golfer arrived at the country club for his usual Saturday round of poor golf. On the third hole he hit a lousy tee shot that landed only fifty yards away. Undeterred, he walked over to his golf bag and pulled out an 8-iron and started to prepare for his second shot. "Excuse me, sir," said the caddie. "You're 247 yards away from the edge of the green. I don't think that's the club you want."

"Listen, kid!" yelled the hacker. "If I had wanted a surveying team to golf with me today, I would have hired one!"

• • •

17. A man came home from his Thursday night golf league, stormed through the front door, threw his clubs down the basement stairs, and swore he'd never golf again. His wife looked at him and said, "You're playing poorly because you have the wrong attitude. You have to be positive when you play. Be positive that you will improve, and things will go much better." The husband calmed down, thanked his wife, and went to the basement to pick up his clubs.

The next week he came home in the same foul mood and did the same thing with his clubs. "What happened to being positive?" she asked.

"Oh, I'm positive, all right," he said tersely. "I'm positive I'll never be a good golfer!"

• • •

18. An avid golfer's teenage son asked for permission to have some friends over on Halloween to watch scary movies and pass out candy. The father agreed and gave him twenty dollars for some videos and snacks. On Halloween night, all the kid's friends came over and seemed to be enjoying themselves. About ten o'clock, however, his parents were scared half out of their wits by violent screaming and shouts coming from the TV room. They dashed upstairs to find out what was wrong.

"What's the matter?!" shouted the father, out of breath. "The movies can't be *that* scary!"

"Movies?" said the son. "They were all lame. We're watching a video of your latest golf game!"

• • •

19. A new member of a posh country club wanted to make a good first impression, so he invited the club pro out for a round of golf. After a decent round, the new member said to the pro, "Thanks for joining me today. It was important to me to prove my game to you. I spent twelve thousand dollars on lessons and new clubs before joining this club."

"Is that so?" said the pro. "Then I guess you'll want to meet my brother-in-law."

"Oh, is he a good golfer, too?"

"No," said the pro. "He's a consumer fraud attorney."

• • •

20. A foursome of regulars was caught in a mess of a traffic jam on the road leading to the golf club. If they didn't move soon, they would be late and lose the tee time they had waited three weeks for. One impatient member got out of the car and walked up to see what was wrong. Upon reaching the gate to the golf club, he saw a sign that said CLOSED INDEFINITELY. He asked the guard at the gate why the course was closed and why there were so many bulldozers and steam shovels on the course.

"We had a foursome of hack golfers come in early this morning. It seems they chipped up so much earth that they discovered the two-thousand-year-old ruins of an ancient city buried beneath the course."

• • •

21. An ex-major league baseball player and a golf pro were sitting in the clubhouse discussing sports and having a few drinks. "Boy, did I make a bad career choice," said the baseball player. "I was in the wrong sport all those years."

"What do you mean?" asked the golf pro. "You had a brilliant career in the majors."

"Oh yeah?" said the baseball player. "It took me over twenty years to get two thousand hits in baseball, but I do it in one day on the golf course!"

• • •

22. A terrible golfer who had just had the worst day of his life at work decided to stop at the club for a quick round of golf before going home to dinner. He was miserable and yelled at the caddie right at the start. "If you say anything about my golfing, give me funny looks, or snicker behind my back, I won't tip you *and* I'll make sure that you lose your job," sniped the man. "Got it?"

"Yes, sir," said the caddie.

Things went progressively downhill from there. He lost three balls on the first hole and shot 4 over on the second.

Still seething from work and growing angrier from his poor play, he teed up his ball at the third hole. He took a mighty swing and sent the ball soaring into the woods. The ball bounced off several trees, sending leaves to the ground, glanced off the pro shop, skipped off a large rock, and crashed through the windshield of his own car. The golfer looked over to see the caddie's reaction. "Well, what are you looking at?"

"The most powerful shot I've ever seen!" said the quick-thinking caddie.

• • •

23. A group of beginning golfers arrived at the country club early in the afternoon on a sunny day to play eighteen holes. The caddies knew they were in for a long afternoon when each one of them took over ten strokes on the first hole. They finally arrived on the eighteenth just as the sun was beginning to set. The first three golfers hit their tee shots into some nearby trees. The fourth hit a tee shot that actually stayed on the fairway.

"They're getting longer," said his caddie to the group.

"Aha!" exclaimed the fourth golfer. "You see, my game is improving. The caddie said my shots are getting longer."

"Don't get excited, sir," said the caddie. "I was referring to the shadows."

• • •

24. A golf pro had assembled his beginners class to hand out certificates of merit for learning the basics of golf. "As you progress to the next level, remember that almost anyone can learn to play golf, but it takes practice to be really good at it," said the instructor. He passed out a certificate to every-one except one golfer.

"What about me, sir? Didn't I learn the basics?" said the hacker.

"*Almost* anyone!"

• • •

25. A hack golfer finished his round of golf and headed for the locker room. On his locker was a note from the club pro.

"Aw, man," cried the golfer. "This is crazy!"

"What is it?" asked another golfer.

"The country club is fining me for hitting my caddie with a seven-iron," the guy said.

"You shouldn't be such a poor sport," said the other golfer.

"It's not that," he said. "They said I used the wrong club."

• • •

26. A hack golfer spent twenty years and over five thousand dollars trying to improve his game, but to no avail. One day, after missing yet another easy putt, he snapped and threw his clubs into the pond. He drove home, got out his revolver, pointed it at his head, and pulled the trigger. The bullet missed completely, putting a hole clean through the ceiling and roof.

He started crying, "Damn! I just can't win!"

• • •

27. A hack golfer was out on the links one day, knocking off bark and chewing up sod. His caddie did everything he could not to laugh out loud with each shot. Finally, after watching the golfer put a third consecutive ball in the drink, the caddie burst out laughing.

"Hey, kid!" shouted the golfer. "You'd better shut up before I knock your block off!"

"Yeah, right," laughed the caddie. "You wouldn't know which club to use and would probably miss if you did!"

• • •

28. After another bad round of golf, one in a two-year series, a hack golfer threw his clubs into the trunk and said to his partner, "That's it. I've had enough. I'm going to make an appointment to see a psychiatrist."

"Think it will help improve your game?" asked the friend.

"No!" the guy exclaimed. "I'm going so I can figure out why I'm crazy enough to keep spending so much time and money on this stupid sport!"

• • •

29. Eddie the hack was out on the course and up to his usual tricks of chewing up sod, losing balls, and making his caddie's life miserable. On the thirteenth, he approached the ball in the fairway and yelled at the caddie to hand him a 3-wood.

"Um, excuse me, sir," the caddie started to say.

"Just shut up for once and hand me the three-wood," Eddie snapped.

The caddie obeyed and watched. Eddie paused, then hit a beautiful shot that bounced twice on the fairway and gently rolled into the cup for a 1 under. "You see that, kid?" exclaimed Eddie. "I know what I'm doing."

"Nice shot, sir," said the frustrated caddie. "Too bad it wasn't your ball!"

• • •

30. A guy decided to take up golf. He'd been watching it on television for years and figured, "How hard could it be?" He went to the local golf store and purchased a set of the best clubs, new shoes, a bunch of cool-looking gadgets, and a tam with a little ball on top. He got up early the next morning, drove to the local course, and got a seven A.M. tee time.

At four P.M. he turned to his caddie, who at this point was beyond furious, and said, "So, when do you think I'll be able to use my putter?"

• • •

31. There was a crabby hack golfer who had a habit of cussing out every caddie he employed. One day, while changing in the clubhouse, the golfer heard a bunch of caddies talking about him. "Man, that golfer is an SOB!" said one of the caddies. The golfer immediately ran around the lockers and began screaming at the caddies.

"All right! Which one of you snots called me an SOB!" he demanded.

The club manager heard the commotion and came running into the locker room. "What's going on here?" the manager demanded.

"One of these imps called me an SOB and I want him fired!" the golfer shouted.

"All right," the manager sighed. "Which one of you called this man an SOB?" Silence filled the room. "C'mon. Which one of you did it? If you don't confess, I'll have to reprimand all of you."

Still there was silence.

After a short period, one brave caddie spoke up and said to the manager, "Sir, I'm not the caddie who called that golfer an SOB, but what I want to know is, who called that SOB a golfer?"

• • •

32. A golfer was so ashamed of his game that he only played alone and only played in the early morning. One day he was out playing a typically bad round. He came to the fourth hole and teed up his ball. He reared back and took a hefty swing, missing the ball by a foot and nearly falling down. He planted his feet, reared back again, and took a vicious swing. *Whoosh*—nothing but air. This went on for three more attempts. Just then, a hunter who had been watching him from some nearby woods emerged.

"Hey, buddy, can't you read? This is for golfers only!" yelled the golfer.

The hunter laughed and replied, "I won't say anything if you won't!"

• • •

33. A golfer who had only been playing for about five years decided it was time to test his skill by playing in the club's annual tournament. Not wanting to look bad, two weeks before the tournament he started playing eighteen holes every day. After the two weeks he looked at his caddies and said, "Well, this is as good as it's going to get. What can you tell me about my opponent for the match?"

"He's lousy," said the caddie. "He slices three out of every five in to the trees, throws more sand than a dog burying a bone, and can't putt to save his life."

"Excellent!" said the golfer.

"Well, not exactly," said the caddie. "He's still gonna stomp your ass!"

• • •

34. Four guys had been playing golf every week for five years. Three were pretty good, while one just couldn't seem to get the hang of fairway shots. On the thirteenth hole, the three of them were on the green waiting for the bad golfer to make his way up. "Say, what's with him, anyway?" said one golfer. "You'd think he'd have the hang of it by now. And what's with that big plastic bag he carries around?"

"Are you kidding?" said another. "He keeps his divots in there. In two more months he will have torn up enough earth to resod his backyard!"

• • •

35. Four hacks are sitting around a table at the clubhouse having a few drinks. They're arguing over who has the most stamina for the game, with the winner getting five bucks from the rest.

"I can play eighteen holes, seven days a week," says the first guy.

"Aw, that's nothing," said the second. "I can play eighteen holes five days a week and thirty-six the other two."

"Wimps!" said a third. "I can play thirty-six holes five days a week and not use a cart."

The fourth one stood up and said, "You're all losers. Pay up! I can golf eighteen holes three days a week."

"That's nothing," said the first.

"Without cussing!" said the fourth, collecting the bills.

• • •

36. A guy was interviewing with a club pro to see if he qualified to take the advanced golf lessons that started in the spring. "Tell me," said the pro, "What do you consider to be the hardest shot to make in golf?"

"Well," he thought for a moment. "I've shot from the rough, out of trees, in and out of sand traps, and countless ponds, but I'd have to say the hardest shot is where you hit a tree, bounce off a rock, slam sideways off a parked cart, bounce up on the green, and roll gently into the cup."

"What are you talking about?" the pro asked.

"I did that twenty years ago and haven't done it since. I'd call that one hard shot!" said the golfer.

• • •

37. A hack was out on the links, missing balls, flubbing shots, and cussing a blue streak the whole time. Beyond frustrated the caddie said, "Excuse me, mister, but your problem is that you're addressing the ball improperly."

The man picked up his ball, tossed it into a nearby pond, and said, "As badly as these *&^%$#$ balls are treating me, I've been as polite as I'm going to be!"

• • •

38. A hack golfer with a penchant for making crazy bets was out golfing with two friends one day. He came to a par-4 with a slight dogleg left and said, "I'll bet each of you ten dollars that I can hole out in two shots."

Smelling easy money, they both took his bet. The hack stepped up to the tee, took a mighty swing, and topped the ball, sending it twelve or so yards down the fairway. "Now what?" sniped one of his buddies.

Not to be shown up, the hack golfer looked around for a moment, took a pitching wedge from his bag, and proceeded to hit the ball onto the green next to his fairway, where it rolled into the cup. Walking back to his buddies with his hand out, he said, "I never said which green!"

• • •

39. A golfer had just finished the worst game of his life, one in a continuing series of bad outings. He stormed into the clubhouse, ripped off all his clothes and threw them in the trash, cut up his new golf shoes, and bent every one of his new clubs. "That's it!" he screamed. "I can't take it any more. I'm gonna kill myself!"

With that he stuck his head in a full sink of water in an attempt to drown himself. A few of his golf buddies just laughed. One said, "Hey, John, we're playing thirty-six tomorrow. Care to join us?"

John jerked his head out of the water and said, "What time?"

• • •

40. A posh golf club installed electronic scoring screens so golfers could compare themselves to other golfers. Two guys were discussing their games at the clubhouse. "So how did you line up on the big screen today?"

"Are you kidding?" said the second. "When I keyed in my score, it said, 'You shot a what?'"

• • •

41. A man was on holiday in Europe and decided to check out a local golf course. The club pro paired him with two German businessmen and their translator. The guy was having the worst game of his life, much to the frustration of everyone else. By the eleventh hole he was so frustrated he began swearing at his clubs, "F*&^ing a*&hole!" The other men just stared at him. "How do I say that in German so they'll understand?" he asked.

The translator responded, "Obviously you haven't been listening to your caddie."

• • •

42. Two friends met at the local watering hole for a quick drink after work. "So, how's your golf game these days?" asked the first.

"Pretty damn scary, or so I'm told," said the second.

"That good, eh?" said the first.

"Good? Heck, no," said the second. "My game is so scary that amusement parks in five states want to video my play and use it as part of the House of Terrors exhibit."

• • •

43. A pro golfer was having the worst round of golf he had had in twenty years. What made it even worse was that his caddie wouldn't recognize a 5-iron if it bit him in the rear end. Finally over the edge after shanking a shot on the fifteenth hole, he demanded to see the club ranger.

"I know there's a penalty for throwing a club or ball, but what's the penalty for throwing a $^%#$@ caddie!?!"

• • •

44. A hack golfer was struggling to get through a round, tearing up sod at every turn. Finally, in a fit of frustration after having shanked another worm burner into the woods, the golfer turned to his caddie and said, "I give up. What do you suggest for this shot?"

"How about a few Hail Marys."

• • •

45. A man learning to golf decided to hire a professional golfer to play eighteen holes with him and instruct him on the way. After hacking up every fairway in sight, the golfer asked the pro, "What's my basic problem here?"

The pro looked at him and said, "It's simple; you're standing too close to your ball . . . after you hit it!"

• • •

46. Two guys were playing a round of golf one Sunday morning. Since the course wasn't very busy that morning, they decided that they would adhere strictly to the rules and not improve their lies. On the third hole, the first guy's ball

landed on the edge of the cart path, partially blocked by asphalt. As he reached down to pick up his ball so he could hit it, his friend said, "We agreed that we play by the rules and not improve our lie."

The two debated the matter for quite some time, with the first man losing the argument. So, he went to the cart to get a club. He stood over his ball and took a few practice swings, each time scraping the club on the pavement, taking out chunks of asphalt and sending out sparks. Finally, after several practice swings, he took his shot. The ball took off and landed on the green about four feet from the pin. "Terrific shot!" said his friend. "What club did you use?"

The man smiled, "I used *your* six-iron!"

• • •

47. Four engineers were golfing at the local club. They came to the fifteenth hole, which was a long dogleg right, 450-yard par-4. On the second shot of the hole, the first golfer walked around looking at everything in the area, took out a piece of paper and looked at it, figured something on his calculator, and got set for his shot. He looked at his watch for about thirty seconds and then hit his shot.

The ball went over the fence and bounced off the pavement, collided with the hubcap of a tour bus going sixty miles per hour, and spun wildly back out onto the fairway and onto the green 275 yards away.

His friends all stared in amazement. One of them asked, "How on earth did you do that?"

"Well," he said, "it helps to know the bus schedule."

• • •

48. A golfer had played a pretty good round for the day, when he came to the fifteenth hole, a relatively long par-3. The golfer, feeling rather confident of his ability, said to his caddie, "This looks like a four-wood tee shot and a one putt to me." The caddie obediently handed him the 4-wood, which he topped, sending the ball about fifteen yards into the fairway.

The smiling caddie handed him his putter and said, "And now for one hell of a putt."

• • •

49. A poor golfer argued with his caddie over club selection for most of his weekly round at the local club. On the second shot of the eighteenth hole, with 175 yards to go and facing a stiff wind, the caddie handed the golfer a 4-wood.

The golfer snarled at the caddie, "I think it's a three-iron."

"No, sir, it's definitely a four-wood," said the caddie.

"What do you know?!" said the golfer, grabbing his 3-iron.

The golfer set up for his shot and hit the ball perfectly, placing it about six feet in front of the cup.

"See," said the caddie. "I told you to use the four-wood!"

• • •

50. An avid golfer came home from his usual Saturday round and bragged to his neighbor about having golfed with the club pro. "It was incredible. It was the best golf of my life. And the best part was, at the end of the round there was only a single-digit difference between us."

"What did the pro shoot?" asked the neighbor.

"He shot a sixty-eight," said the golfer.

"You mean *you* shot a sixty-nine?" exclaimed the golfer.

"No. I shot a *one* sixty-eight."

• • •

51. Two friends met for their weekly round of golf. The first one said, "Do you know of a good attorney?"

"Why do you need an attorney?" asked the second.

The first one replied, "I sent a golf club manufacturer a few pictures of me golfing with their equipment in hopes that they would use me in one of their ads."

"So, why do you need an attorney?" asked the second.

"Do you know what an injunction is?"

• • •

52. A hack golfer spent three hours on the front nine and was on pace for another three to finish. His caddie, while polite, was growing impatient with each flubbed shot. After seventeen grueling holes, the golfer was determined to smash the ball off the eighteenth tee. He wound up, took a mighty swing at the ball, and said, "Wow! Look at that sucker go. Did you see that?"

"Hate to disappoint you, sir, but that was your wristwatch. You missed the ball completely!"

• • •

53. A golfer of three months was at the local course for a round of golf. As usual, he was tearing up sod and missing putts. After blowing his putt on the thirteenth hole he said to his caddie, "Damn, I want to be a golfer in the worst way."

The disgusted caddie said, "If you stop now, you'll be way ahead of yourself."

• • •

54. A guy came home after his round of golf, tossed his clubs in the garage, and promptly slammed the door.

"How did you do today?" his wife asked.

"Good and bad," said the husband. "I got a hole in one on the fifth hole."

"What could possibly be bad about that?"

"I still shot a 135 for the day."

• • •

DOCTORS AND LAWYERS

55. A lawyer is ready to tee off when a golfer in an adjacent fairway hits him square in the face with his golf ball. "You idiot! Your ball hit me in the eye! I'll sue you for five million bucks!"

The other golfer replies, "I said, 'Fore!'"

The lawyer says, "I'll take it!"

• • •

56. A priest, a doctor, and a lawyer are waiting to start their golf game one morning, but are held up by a particularly slow group of golfers.

The lawyer says, "What's with these guys? We've been waiting for over fifteen minutes!"

The doctor says, "I don't know, but someone should tell the ranger!"

The priest says, "Hey, here comes the ranger now. Let's have a word with him." He turns to the ranger. "Say, not to complain, but what's with that group ahead of us? They're rather slow."

The ranger says, "Oh, yes, that's a group of blind fire-fighters. They lost their sight saving our clubhouse from a terrible fire last year, so we always let them play anytime for free."

The group falls silent for a moment.

The priest says, "That's so sad. I will say a special prayer for them tonight."

The doctor says, "Good idea. I'll call my ophthalmologist buddy and see if there's anything he can do for them."

The lawyer says, "Why can't these guys play at night?"

• • •

57. A lawyer was enjoying a quiet round of golf by himself one morning. When he approached the tee on the seventh hole, he thought he heard faint cries for help. The closer he got to the green, the louder the cries were. He walked over to a rather large, deep bunker next to the green and saw a man who had accidentally driven in and was trapped underneath his overturned golf cart.

"Go get some help," the man said.

"Did anyone see you drive in?" the lawyer asked.

"No one," grunted the man.

"Great," the lawyer said, jumping in. "Move over!"

• • •

58. A doctor and a lawyer met up in the clubhouse after a round of golf. The doctor said, "Hey, how's your golf game these days?"

"Not bad. I'm finally shooting in the mid-seventies," said the lawyer.

"Honestly?" the doctor asked.

"What's that got to do with it?"

• • •

59. A golfer was rushed to the emergency room from the golf course one day. It seems he was choking to death on a golf ball that was caught in his throat. He was immediately taken into an operating room, followed by a team of surgeons and specialists. Just then a lawyer ran up to the nurse's station and frantically asked about the man's condition.

"How's he doing?" asked the lawyer. "Will the procedure take very long?"

"Oh, you must be one of the family members," said the nurse.

"No, that's my ball, and they're waiting for me on eleven!"

• • •

60. A golfer was asked to join a regular threesome one Sunday morning to keep the game play moving quickly. As he got ready to putt at the first hole, one of the guys started rocking from side to side. "Excuse me, but would you mind not doing that in my sight line?" asked the golfer. The guy stopped.

The golfer reset for his shot, but missed the putt. He walked off the green frowning. At the second green, he set up for his putt, but the other guy started rocking from side to side again. "Hey!" said the golfer. "Do you mind? I'm trying to putt for par here." Once again the guy stopped rocking.

This went on for two more holes, until finally the golfer lost control. "What in the hell are you doing that for?" he asked.

"I'm sorry, pal, but I'm at sea three weeks out of four," said the guy. "I just got into port yesterday and haven't gotten my land legs yet."

"That's no excuse! I'm a lawyer who just finished a big trial, but you don't see me running around trying to screw everyone!"

• • •

61. Two dads were in the waiting room of the maternity ward, waiting for a chance to see their new sons in the nursery. The first one said, "So, what's your son going to be when he grows up?"

"What? How should I know?" said the second. "He's only four hours old."

"I've got my son's life already planned," said the first. "He's going to be a successful doctor or dentist."

"How can you be sure that he'll grow up to be a doctor?" asked the second.

"Simple. I went out this morning and purchased him a set of Ping golf clubs."

• • •

62. A doctor, an artist, and a lawyer were having lunch and a few drinks at the clubhouse one day when the conversation turned to their respective dogs. Each thought his dog was more intelligent than the others', so they made a bet to see who was right.

The doctor decided to go first. "Hippocrates! Fetch, boy!" And with that the doctor's dog ran outside, sniffed for a few minutes, and promptly dug up a complete human skeleton, which he reassembled in front of the trio. The dog was rewarded with some hamburger.

The artist said, "That's nothing. Botticelli! Do your stuff!" The artist's dog then began chewing the bones to pulp, and transformed the mess into a version of *The Birth of Venus*. The dog was rewarded with some rib bones.

"Kid's stuff," said the lawyer. "Cochran! Fresh meat!" The lawyer's dog darted over to the other two dogs and stole their treats, nipped at the doctor and artist, sold the artwork for a huge fee, then proceeded to go out and play a round of golf.

• • •

63. Two beautiful female golfers met at their club for a quick round of golf after work. Ahead of them was a pair of male lawyers. The lawyers wanted to meet the women, so they decided to slow their play, forcing the women to catch up to them. Sure enough, by the fifth hole the women were right up with them. The lawyers asked if the women would like to join them, to which one replied, "Not on your life. We don't golf with lawyers!"

Well, that comment fractured the ego of one of the lawyers, so he hatched a plan. "On the next hole, when the women hit their balls toward us, you lie down and pretend you were hit. We'll sue those broads for a million bucks," said the first lawyer.

Sure enough, a golf ball came bouncing up to one of the lawyer's feet. He immediately lay down and waited for the women to approach them. "Now look what you've done," said the first lawyer. "You smacked my friend in the temple and now he's probably going to die. We're going to sue you for ten million dollars."

"Oh, why don't you kiss my @#%," said one of the women.

"Hey, get up. They want to settle out of court."

• • •

OLD DUFFERS

---

64. An avid golfer had been playing golf at the local club for over fifty years and recently began having trouble with his eyes. He walked into the office at the club one day and said, "I've come to let you know that I've decided to resign my membership this year."

"I'm very sorry to hear that," said the club pro. "What's the problem?"

"Well, it's the damn eyesight, you know," he explained. "At seventy-nine it's getting so that I can't see where my shots land, even with the strongest glasses available. It's a complete waste of time."

"Don't worry," said the pro. "We have a new member who's eighty-six and he's got twenty–twenty eyesight. He doesn't even wear glasses. I'll pair him with you next week when you golf, and he can keep an eye on your ball for you."

"Hey, that's great," the man replied. "Thanks!"

So, there they were the next Monday morning, on the first tee. The old guy stepped up to the tee and hit his drive. "Wow, what a smack. Did you see it?"

"Oh yeah, I saw it."

"Where did it go?"

"Where did what go?"

• • •

65. One day an old duffer challenged the local young golf pro to a match, with a $1,000 bet on the side.

"I have one condition on the match and the bet," said the duffer. "You're obviously much better than I am, so to even it a bit you have to spot me two 'gotchas.' "

The golf pro had no idea what a "gotcha" was, but he went along with it. Coming back to the clubhouse, the rest of the club members were amazed to see the golf pro paying the duffer $1,000.

"What happened?" asked one of the members.

"Well," said the pro, "I was teeing up for the first hole, and as I brought the club down, the old man stuck his hand up between my legs, grabbed my balls, and yelled, 'Gotcha!' Have you ever tried to play eighteen holes of golf waiting for the second 'gotcha'?"

• • •

66. Four old friends have been playing golf for years, but one of them is a terrible whiner. One day the whiner dies on the course after complaining about a missed putt. A funeral service is held, and as the pallbearers are carrying out the coffin at the end of the service, they bump into a wall, rocking the casket. Someone says he heard a sound come from inside the casket. They open it up, and, sure enough, the guy is still alive. He lives, golfs, and whines ten more years, then dies for good.

Another ceremony is held, and at the end the pallbearers start carrying out the coffin. As they're walking out, one of the golf pals calls out, "Watch out for the wall!"

• • •

67. A wife begins to get a little worried because her husband has not arrived home on time from his regular Saturday afternoon golf game. As the hours pass she becomes more and more concerned until, at eight P.M., the husband finally pulls into the driveway.

"Where the heck have you been?" the wife exclaims. "You should have been home hours ago!"

"Larry had a heart attack on the fifth hole," the husband explains.

"Oh, that's terrible," the wife says.

"I know," says the husband. "All day long it was hit the ball, drag Larry, hit the ball, drag Larry . . ."

• • •

68. Two old friends were enjoying a round of golf, but one kept losing his ball. The first guy reaches into his golf bag and pulls out a green ball. He hands it to his friend and says, "Hey, why don't you try this ball? You can't lose it."

His friend replies, "What do you mean you can't lose it?!"

The first man replies, "It's a special ball. If you hit it into the woods it makes a beeping sound, if you hit it into the water it produces bubbles, and if you hit it on the fairway, smoke comes up in order for you to find it."

His friend is amazed at all the features of this golf ball. "Wow! That's incredible! Where did you get that ball?"

His friend says, "I found it."

• • •

69. Two old duffers had been friends for over sixty years, hardly ever missing a golf date on Saturday. One day one of the duffers turned to his friend and said, "Let's make a

promise that whoever dies first, he'll come back and tell the other whether there's golf in heaven." They agreed.

A few weeks later one of the old duffers died. The other one continued to play golf, but it wasn't the same. Then one Saturday on the eighth hole, the old duffer saw his friend standing next to him.

"Charlie? Charlie? Is it really you?" the first duffer said.

"Yes, it's really me. I kept my promise."

"Well, what's it like? Is there plenty of golf?"

"Well, I'm afraid I have good news and bad news," said Charlie. "The good news is, there's all the free golf you want and all the free lessons you can handle. The bad news is, you're due to tee off next Saturday!"

• • •

70. Two old duffers head out for a quick round of golf. Since it is late in the day, they decide to play only nine holes. The first duffer says, "Let's say we make it interesting and spot five dollars on the lowest score for the day." The other duffer agrees and they enjoy a great game. After the eighth hole, the first old duffer is ahead by one stroke, but cuts his ball into the rough on the ninth.

The first old duffer says, "Help me find my ball. You look over there; I'll look over here." After about fifteen minutes neither has any luck finding the ball. A lost ball carries a four-point penalty, and it's getting late, so the first old duffer secretly pulls a ball from his pocket and tosses it to the ground. "I've found my ball!" he says.

The second old duffer looks at him and frowns. "Man alive. After all the years we've been friends, you'd cheat me on golf for a measly five bucks?"

"What do you mean, cheat? I found my ball sitting right here."

"First a cheat and now a liar!" the second old duffer says. "I'll have you know, I've been standing on your ball for the last five minutes!"

• • •

71. Two old friends decide to go golfing on a hot Wednesday afternoon. On the seventh hole the first guy collapses on the green. His friend shouts out for assistance. Two doctors playing on the sixth hole quickly drive their cart to help the man. The first doctor takes out his emergency kit, examines the man, and says, "I'm sorry, but your friend's dead."

"It can't be," says the man. "He's in perfect health. I want a second opinion."

The second doctor goes to his golf cart, pulls a small cat from his golf bag, and places it near the dead man's feet. The cat sniffs a bit, walks around the man, sniffs a little more, then sits down and meows at the doctor.

"What does it mean?" the man asks.

"He says your friend is dead," the doctor replies.

"I can't believe it," says the man in tears. "How much do I owe you?"

"That'll be three hundred and fifty dollars," one of the doctors says.

"What! Where do you get off charging me three hundred and fifty dollars to tell me my friend's dead?" exclaims the man in disbelief.

"Well," says the first doctor, "the diagnosis was fifty dollars, and it's three hundred dollars for the cat scan."

• • •

72. Four old friends meet at the local public course for a round of golf each week. One of the guys shows up wearing a new pair of glasses. At the first green he sinks a twenty-five-foot putt. His friends are amazed. On the second green he sinks another long-distance putt, again to his friends' amazement.

One guy says, "Hey, you're really on fire today. What's your secret?"

"Aha! It's these new bifocals," says the golfer. "With these I see a small ball and a big ball. I always aim for the large one, and the rest is history."

On the fifth hole, the golfer needs to relieve himself and heads off into some nearby woods. When he returns, his trousers are completely soaked.

"Land sakes, what happened to you?" one of the golfers asks.

"I'm not quite sure. I looked down and saw a big one and a little one. I knew the big one wasn't mine, so I put it back!"

• • •

73. A foursome was playing a round of golf after work. One of the players was a true hack and was slowing the whole game down. Finally, one golfer took him aside and said, "Look, pal, maybe you should give up golf and take up checkers. It's more your speed."

After the game, the guy thought about it and joined a local checkers club. He was playing a slow game when the other guy said, "Say, bud. You're overthinking this game. Have you ever considered taking up golf?"

• • •

74. Two young caddies assigned to two old duffers knew they were in for a long day on the course. After failing to hit the ball for the umpteenth time, one duffer turned to his caddie and said, "I suppose you've never seen a player worse than me?"

The caddie quipped, "Oh, I've seen plenty worse than you, but they're all dead!"

• • •

75. An older member of a prestigious country club came into the clubhouse after his usual eighteen holes and complained that he was having more and more trouble getting out of the bunkers. The pro suggested a number of helpful strategies, to which the old man retorted, "You don't understand. It's not the ball that's troubling me. It is getting myself out!"

• • •

76. An old duffer had golfed at the same country club with his friends for over sixty years. He took ill and died suddenly, leaving the rest of his group to mourn. In his will he requested that his ashes be scattered on the green of the club's toughest hole, number fifteen, a long par-4 with a dogleg left and a huge bunker. His wife and golf buddies all thought that it was odd that in all the years he played at the club, he had always ended up in the bunker and never on the green. But, this way, he could always say in heaven that he made the green on fifteen.

On the day of his funeral everyone gathered at the fifteenth green to say their final goodbyes. It was a warm, calm, sunny day without a cloud in the sky. As the preacher finished his eulogy and his wife began pouring the ashes out of the urn, a freak gust of wind rose up over the green catching the ashes, carrying them to the bunker. "Boy, he still can't get a break on this hole!" said one of his golf buddies.

• • •

77. Two old friends bumped into each other at the clubhouse after a round of golf. "Hey, how are you? I haven't seen you in months. How's the golf game?" said the first guy.

The second guy said, "Well, I can't complain today. I shot a three-under on the eighteenth."

"Wait a minute," said the second guy. The eighteenth is a 415-yard par-four with a dogleg right. How could you possibly hit three-under?"

"It's simple," the first guy said with a laugh. "One under a tree, one under the cart, and one under the clubhouse!"

• • •

78. A golfer of fifty-two years was told by his doctor that his arthritis was so bad that he couldn't golf anymore. Wanting desperately to remain near the game, he asked the doctor if he could caddie using wheeled bags. The doctor said sure, and off the old guy went to be a caddie. About three days

later the doctor spotted the old guy greeting people at the local super market. "Hey, what happened to your caddie job?" the doctor asked.

"Got fired," the old man mumbled.

"Were you late for work?" asked the doctor.

"Nope."

"Arguing with the golfers?"

"Nope."

"Sleeping on the job?"

"Nope."

"Then what was it?" asked the doctor.

"I couldn't stop laughing!"

• • •

79. An old golfer at the country club was notorious for being a skinflint, and none of the caddies liked working for him. When he pulled into the lot for his usual daily round of golf, the caddies argued about who would have to put up with him that day. Finally, one spoke up, "Hey, go inside and get the new guy. He doesn't know how this guy is." So the old golfer and the new caddie walked to the first tee.

"Before we begin, I need to know that you're the best at finding lost balls," said the old guy.

"Rest assured, sir. I am the best lost-ball finder in the entire caddie crew," boasted the young caddie, eager to please.

"Great," said the old guy. "Go find a quick two dozen so we can get started!"

• • •

80. Two old duffers were at the clubhouse going on and on about golf and sex. A young golfer at the next table leaned over and said, "You know, it's amazing how at your ages you can spend so much time just talking about golf and sex."

One old duffer quipped, "Sonny, at our ages, all we *can* do is talk about it!"

• • •

81. There was an old duffer who liked to play a round of golf every Saturday morning before taking his wife out for shopping and lunch. Since he only lived a few blocks from the golf course he would wheel his bag there rather than drive. One Saturday morning while on his way to the course he noticed a group of older neighborhood boys carrying golf bags, obviously on their way to the course for some fun. Then he saw a younger boy sitting on the curb crying his eyes out. "Say, young man," said the duffer, "what seems to be the problem?"

The young boy looked up, wiped his eyes, and sobbed, "I'm crying because I can't do what the big boys do."

The old man thought for a moment, then sat down next to him and started crying with him.

• • •

82. An old duffer and a young golfer were paired at the Reflections course at Garland one Sunday morning. Both were decent golfers, and the game was moving along at a good pace. Throughout the first nine holes the young golfer was amazed that the old duffer could play so well without taking the time to line up his shots or take practice swings. "You're amazing," said the young golfer. "You go right up to the ball, don't waste a lot of time, don't take a practice swing, and yet you're a pretty good golfer."

"Well, sonny," said the duffer. "At my age you have no time or swings to waste!"

• • •

83. Two old duffers were in the clubhouse having a few drinks and discussing their games. "You know, kids today don't have any sense of doing things the right way," said the first duffer.

"What do you mean?" the second asked.

"I was paired up with two hack twenty-somethings the other day, and after each shot they would throw their clubs every which direction," said the first.

"But I see you do that all the time," the second pointed out.

"Yeah, but at least I know enough to throw mine in the right direction!"

• • •

84. Two old friends were out on the course early one morning. They had played a great match, going to the eighteenth tied. Both had terrific drives and were on the green in two. The first old guy's ball lay about ten feet from the hole. The second old guy's ball lay six feet from the hole, on the same line. The first old guy lined up his putt, gently tapped the ball, and watched as it rolled directly to the hole, lipped the cup, and rolled left about a foot. "Ha! You missed," said the second old guy. So the second old guy lined up his shot, tapped the ball, and got the same result.

"Looks like you screwed up the same shot!" snapped the first old guy.

"Yeah, well, I learned from the master," said the second.

• • •

85. A cheap old duffer is reading the local sports page and sees an ad offering golf balls for half price. At nine o'clock the duffer drives to the store and walks up to the salesman.

"Excuse me, sonny, do you have any golf balls?" he asks.

"Gee, I'm sorry, sir," says the salesman. "The sale has been on for two days and we're fresh out. We're expecting a new supply tomorrow morning. I'll set two sleeves aside for you."

"Great," says the duffer, walking out.

At ten o'clock the same guy appears and walks up to the salesman. "Excuse me, sonny, do you have any golf balls?"

"Ah, no, sir," he says. "As I said earlier, we're fresh out. How about I save you three sleeves tomorrow?"

"Great," says the duffer, walking out again.

At eleven o'clock the same guy walks in and goes to the same salesman. "Excuse me, sonny, do you have any golf balls?"

The salesman is irked. "Now, look, buddy. I told you at nine and ten that I didn't have any golf balls. It's eleven now, and I still don't have any. Please, stop asking. I have a lot of work to do."

"Excellent," says the duffer, walking out once more.

The salesman is getting a little paranoid, and by noon starts to look at his watch. Sure enough, the old duffer comes in and asks, "Excuse me, sonny, do—"

Before he can finish the salesman cuts him off, screaming, "Look, pal, can you spell bat, as in baseball bat?"

"Yes, B-A-T," says the duffer.

"Can you spell pong, as in Ping-Pong?"

"Sure, P-O-N-G," says the duffer.

"Then, can you spell freak, as in golf balls?"

"Wait a minute," says the duffer. "There's no freak in golf balls."

"That's what I'm tryin' to tell ya, mister. *There ain't no freakin' golf balls!*"

• • •

86. Four old duffers were sitting around bemoaning their decreasing golfing abilities.

"I used to hit the ball 250 yards easily, and now I'm lucky if I can hit it 150," said the first.

"Yeah, time was when I could fade the ball around trees, but not anymore," said the second.

"I miss the good putting game I used to have," said the third.

The fourth guy was silent. "What about you? What do you miss the most?" asked the third.

"Who, me? Any shot I can *find* makes me happy!"

• • •

87. A little old man was paired with two so-so golfers one Saturday morning. To the surprise of the younger golfers, the little old man kept right up with them. On the ninth hole, a long par-3, the young guys hit decent shots, but the little old man hit into some nearby trees. Before proceeding to their balls, they all spoke to their caddies.

"I'll take a seven-iron," said the first young guy.

"I'll take an eight," said the second.

"I'll take a sweater," sighed the little old man. "It's going to be a while!"

• • •

88. Old duffer no. 1: "Damn! This grip is too loose. It's affecting my whole game."

Old duffer no. 2: "Why don't you go to the pro shop and get your clubs regripped?"

Old duffer no. 1: "Who said anything about clubs? I was talking about my dentures. Every time I tee off, they fly halfway out of my mouth!"

• • •

89. Two old duffers were out on the course one day when one said, "Ya know, life just isn't fair sometimes."

"How do you mean?" the second asked.

"Now that I can finally afford to buy the best golf balls instead of using scrubs, I'm not able to hit them far enough to lose them!"

• • •

90. First duffer: "What do you miss about being a young golfer?"

Second duffer: "Hitting for distance, hitting it accurately, and, uh, er, umm . . . I forget!"

• • •

91. An old duffer gentleman lived on the third floor of a retirement condo on a golf course and used the cart path to walk to the corner grocery. One day, as he was returning from the store, he looked down and saw that beside a tree next to the path were dozens of brand-new golf balls. He couldn't believe his good fortune! The man put as many as he could inside the paper bag, and the rest in his pockets, making them bulge. He returned to his condo and waited for the elevator. When the elevator door opened, an elderly lady with an elastic bandage wrapped around one of her elbows stepped out. She looked at his bulging pockets with obvious curiosity.

Embarrassed, the old duffer said, "Golf balls."

The elderly lady pointed to her elbow and said, "Tennis elbow."

• • •

92. First old duffer: "My game's improving. Today I came pretty darn close to getting a hole-in-one."

Second old duffer: "Oh yeah, how close was it?"

First old duffer: "Three strokes and twenty yards."

• • •

93. Two old golf buddies were on the back nine one day complaining about getting older. "Man, these hills are getting steeper as the years go by," said the first one. "And the fairways seem to be getting longer, too."

"The sand traps seem to be bigger than I remember them, too," said the second one.

A little time went by and the first one declared, "At eighty-five I'm just thankful we're still on the right side of the grass!"

• • •

94. Two young men stopped at the local municipal course for a quick nine holes before going home. They had been held up for about twenty minutes on the third hole when the course ranger drove up to them and asked, "What's the problem, fellas?"

"It's this old guy—he's taking forever," said one of the golfers.

The ranger looked over at the old guy and smiled. "Oh, that's Old Bill. He's been around forever. He comes out every day for a round of golf. Everybody likes Old Bill."

"Gee, how old is he?" asked the other golfer.

"No one really knows for sure, but his handicap is in Roman numerals."

• • •

95. Fred and Paul had been playing golf together for over forty years, and Fred always beat Paul. Now Paul was to move with his wife to a senior community in Florida, so the two

old friends decided to meet for one last game. Paul was playing unusually well and headed to the eighteenth tied with his longtime partner. He teed up his ball, closed his eyes, and said, "Dear Lord, please, just this once, let me hit this ball with the strength and skill of a professional. This is my last game with Fred, and I have to beat him at least once."

Satisfied with his stance, he pulled back his club and swung with enough force to knock himself to the ground. He looked up in time to see his ball slice wildly off course, smack into the clubhouse door, carom off two cars, hit a rock, and gently roll onto the green. He looked up at the sky and said, "Nice going, Lord. I'll take it from here."

• • •

4

HAZARDS

---

96. A nerdy lawyer decided to take up golf as a hobby to try to fit in with his peers, since golf was all they talked about at meetings. He bought all the appropriate gear and decided to take some lessons before joining his friends on the links. On about the fourth lesson, the club pro suggested they play a round of golf to get a better feel for the game.

Everything seemed to be going along fine until they came to the sixth hole, a par-3, 190-yard shot that had to travel over water to a little island where the green was located. The lawyer looked at the pro in utter confusion and said, "Assuming I can even get the ball on the little island, how the heck am I supposed to get out there to finish the hole?"

"Good question," replied the pro. "You can either use the rowboat provided by the course or if you don't mind getting wet, you can walk out. The water's only two feet deep."

"Oh, I get it now," said the lawyer. "It's row versus wade!"

• • •

97. A novice golfer plays the local **public** course every week and always seems to have trouble with the water trap on the twelfth hole, losing two or three balls every time he plays it. On one round he gets smart and decides to use an old cut-up ball he found the week before. He opens his bag, gets the old ball, tees it up, and gets ready to swing. Just as his backswing is in motion, a mighty voice from the heavens decrees, *"Use the new ball."*

He is shocked and figures any advice from God should be followed. He picks up the old ball and tees up a new one. He starts his backswing, but once again is interrupted by a voice from heaven, *"Take a practice swing."*

The man steps away from the ball, takes a practice swing, and just as he steps forward to readdress the ball, the voice speaks again, *"Use the old ball."*

• • •

98. A lousy golfer decided to play eighteen holes one Saturday morning. He hit every sand trap on the course and by the sixteenth hole his caddie was getting quite upset with how long the round was taking. Sure enough, on seventeen, the guy smacked the ball directly into the sand trap. After sizing up his situation the golfer said, "Do you think I can get there with an eight-iron?"

"Sure, eventually!"

• • •

99. An old duffer hit his tee shot from the fifth hole into a water hazard. Frustrated, he walked over to look for his ball and saw it about six feet from the shore in some shallow water. He took his ball retriever from his bag and reached out into the water and got his ball. As he was drying off the ball and retriever, he heard a small raspy voice speak to him.

"Hey, mister," said the voice.

He looked around and didn't see anyone. He walked back to drop his ball along the ball's line of play for his penalty when he heard the voice again. "Pssst. Hey, mister."

The guy poked around in the weeds and grass by the water and saw a frog. "Hey, mister," said the frog.

"Uh, you're a talking frog? What do you want?" asked the old duffer.

"Mister. Today's your lucky day. I'm really a beautiful princess, but a wicked old witch put a spell on me and turned me into an ugly frog. If you'll pick me up and kiss me, I'll turn back into a beautiful princess and we can go to your house and make wild, passionate love for hours," said the frog.

The man looked around to see that no one was looking, reached down and picked up the frog, and put it in the pocket of his windbreaker. He walked a few yards back down the fairway and prepared for his shot.

"Hey, mister. Aren't you going to kiss me?"

The old duffer, took the frog out of his pocket, looked at it, and thought for a moment. "No, I don't think so. At my age, I think I'd rather have a talking frog!"

• • •

100. A golfer walks into the pro shop, looks around for a while, and starts to frown. Finally the pro shop manager asks him what he's looking for. "I can't seem to find any green golf balls," the golfer replies.

The manager looks all over the shop, thumbs through all the catalogs, and finally calls the manufacturers. "I'm sorry, sir," says the manager. "There aren't any green golf balls available anywhere."

Just as the golfer is about to walk out the door the manager asks him, "Excuse me, sir, why were you looking for green golf balls?"

The golfer says, "Well, obviously, because they're so much easier to find in the sand traps!"

• • •

101. The head ranger at an exclusive private golf club came running into the president's office and said that he had just seen one of the club's longtime members making love to the club secretary in a sand bunker on the ninth hole. "He should be thrown out of this club immediately," said the irate ranger.

"Nonsense," said the president. "I can't think of a male member of this club who wouldn't want to do the same. It's no reason for throwing him out."

"Yes, but he didn't rake the bunker afterward!"

• • •

102. A man was playing a round of golf with his priest and was trying to be extra careful about the language he used. On the eleventh hole he landed in a sand bunker. After three shots he still couldn't get the ball out and let loose with a string of expletives. The priest looked at him calmly and said, "It's been my experience that the best golfers do not use foul language."

"I guess not," said the man. "What the hell do they have to cuss about?"

• • •

103. Two friends were playing a round of golf on a Saturday morning. They came to the sixth hole, which was a long par-4 with water to the right and a deep ravine to the left. The first guy took out a brand-new sleeve of balls, teed one up, and promptly hit it into the water. Undaunted, he pulled another ball from the sleeve and hit that one into the water as well. Then he took the last ball from the sleeve and hit it directly into the water. With a sigh, he then reached into his bag and pulled out a second sleeve of new balls.

"Why don't you hit an old ball?" asked the second man.

The first guy responded, "I've never had an old ball."

• • •

104. Two Scotsmen, Angus and Thomas, were playing at St. Andrews one day and came upon a water hole. Thomas hit

his ball and sent it into the middle of the pond. He reached into his bag and found that he had no more golf balls. He asked Angus for a ball and promptly hit that one into the pond as well.

This went on three or four more times, and when he asked Angus for a sixth ball, Angus said, "Thomas, these balls cost me money, you know."

Thomas replied, "Angus, lad, if ya canna afford to play the game, ya shouldn't be oot here."

• • •

105. Tom and Mike were enjoying a peaceful round of golf one Friday afternoon. On the tenth hole Tom sliced his tee shot into a heavily wooded ravine. He took his 8-iron and proceeded down the steep embankment into the ravine to look for his ball. While he was searching he saw something shiny on the ground. As he approached the object, he realized that it was an 8-iron in the hands of a skeleton lying near an old golf ball. Tom screamed, "Hey, Mike, you gotta come down here and see this one."

Mike came running over to the edge of the ravine and shouted, "What's the matter? What'd you find?"

Tom called back, "I'll put it to you this way. You'd better bring me my seven-iron. I'll never get out of here with an eight."

• • •

106. A golfer is playing a round of golf with his buddies at a posh country club. He isn't doing very well but is controlling his anger so as not to embarrass himself. They come up to the fourth hole, which has water hazards on both sides. Sure enough, he proceeds to duff nine new balls into the water. Frustrated over his poor golfing ability, he lets out a stream of curse words, heaves his Ping golf clubs into the water, and begins to walk off the course.

All of a sudden he turns around and jumps in the lake where he threw his clubs. His buddies joke that he must be going in to retrieve his clubs. When he comes out of the water without his clubs and begins walking toward the clubhouse, one of his buddies asks, "Why did you jump into the lake and not bring out your clubs?"

The golfer screams, "I left my ^%#@**$ car keys in the bag!"

• • •

107. A golfer and his caddie were on the twelfth hole at a posh golf resort in Florida. It was a long par-3 with water on both sides of the green. "You know," said the caddie, "last week I caddied the pro tour and on this shot they all used—"

"Yeah, yeah," said the golfer, cutting him off. "Skip it."

The golfer lost four balls in the water trying to get on the green. "All right, kid. You win. What did the pros use?" he asked.

"An old ball!"

• • •

108. A decent golfer was paired with a hack golfer one morning by the course ranger. The hack golfer never shut up, complaining about everything. "The course is too narrow, the grass is too high, the signs are incorrect . . ." and on and on. On the sixteenth hole, a long par-3 with a large bunker on either side, both golfers hit their tee shots into the sand. The hack golfer yapped and yapped all the way to the bunker. After climbing into the bunker and taking five shots, the hack golfer said, "This is the biggest, deepest, most annoying trap ever!"

"You're absolutely right about that," said the second golfer. "Maybe it's time you kept it shut for a while!"

• • •

109. A hack golfer called the golf club to make reservations for Saturday. After taking the reservation the club pro told one of his assistants to call the National Guard and tell them to meet them on sixteen.

"Why do we need the National Guard?" asked the assistant.

"That hole has a water hazard. The last time he played it, he sunk so many golf balls he flooded the basements in two counties!"

• • •

110. Golfer no. 1: "The water hazard on fourteen isn't going to steal my ball today!"

Golfer no. 2: "What are you going to do, skip the hole?"

Golfer no. 1: "No way. I bought an experimental golf ball that's designed for water play. It's made out of bicarbonate. If it lands in the water, I either watch for bubbles or listen for fish farts."

• • •

111. A guy showed up for his weekly golf game with his four-some, carrying a little dog. One of the guys said, "What the heck are you doing with that dog?"

"Who, Eddie here?" said the golfer. "You guys know I have a bad habit of hitting a ton of balls into the hazards around here. I've trained Eddie to find them and show me where they are after I hit them."

On the first tee, the guy hit a wicked slice into some nearby trees. He told Eddie to go find the ball. A few seconds later, Eddie came out of the trees and barked once.

"What does that mean?" asked another golfer.

"That means he found one ball," said the guy.

On the fourth hole, the guy flubbed a fairway shot that landed in a small pond. Eddie immediately ran after it and dived into the water. A few minutes he came out of the water and barked twice.

"What does that mean?" asked yet another golfer.

"That means he found two balls this time," said the guy.

On the eleventh hole the guy hooked a shot deep into the trees. Eddie took off and seemed to be gone for a long time. Finally, he reappeared, ran up to the guy with a stick in his mouth, and began humping the guy's leg while shaking his head.

"What the hell does that mean?" asked the fourth golfer.

47

"It means there's more F&^%ing golf balls in there than you can shake a stick at!"

• • •

112. Two friends met up in the clubhouse one day after a round of golf. "So how'd you do today?" asked the first.

"Put it this way: I landed in so many sand traps and took so many strokes getting out, I'm thinking of changing my name to Lawrence of Arabia!"

• • •

113. A man was on vacation in Africa and was driving along in his Jeep when he came upon a golf course. Happening to have his clubs with him, he decided to ask whether he could play a round. The pro told him that it was okay, as long as the man used one of the local caddies. The man agreed and left with his caddie. Everything was going fine until the fourth fairway when, all of a sudden, a lion ran out of the jungle toward the man. Seeing this, the caddie quickly pulled out a rifle and shot the lion dead before it reached the man.

"Now I understand why I need you!" exclaimed the man to the caddie.

As they approached the ninth tee, a leopard leapt toward the man from the undergrowth. Once again, the caddie pulled out his trusty rifle and killed the animal, and they moved on.

Three holes later the man was about to play his putt on the twelfth green when a crocodile came out of a large pond and promptly bit off the man's leg. Writhing around on the ground in agony the man angrily asked his caddie why on earth he hadn't got his rifle out again, to which the caddie replied, "Sorry, sir, you don't get a shot on this hole!"

• • •

114. First golfer: "Man, this is the toughest course I've ever played."

Second golfer: "How would you know? You played the whole course from the rough!"

• • •

5

INSULTS

115. A foursome met at their country club for a round of golf one morning. One of the foursome had just purchased a Great Big Bertha and was bragging about how he was going to beat the other three on drives. "You fellas are in for it today. I'm gonna air-mail my balls all day long."

Another of the foursome, irritated with his boasting, said, "You can air-mail balls all day, but that won't help your game. Your problem is you can't get the balls to the right zip code!"

• • •

116. Golfer to his partner who just lost another ball in the water hazard: "Too bad you don't sink putts as well as you sink your drives!"

• • •

117. He holds up play so much that if you were to look up the word *slow* in the dictionary you'd see his picture!

• • •

118. A guy just spent five hundred dollars on new golf attire. "Get a load of me, guys," he said. "I look just like the Shark!"

One of his buddies replied, "You may look like the Shark, but you still play like a minnow!"

• • •

119. A slow golfer was getting lip from his caddie all day when he finally broke. "That's it, you little brat. I've had enough of your lip. I'm gonna have you fired when we get back to the clubhouse."

"Are you kidding?!" said the caddie. "I'll be *retired* by the time we get back!"

• • •

120. Two guys are paired up for a round of golf. The first one says, "I hope you can keep up with me; I'm known as a scratch golfer."

The second guy replies, "Yeah, I hear you should be scratched from the club's roster!"

• • •

121. That guy is such a lousy golfer that when he yells "Fore" no one knows whether he's telling people to duck or counting the people he just hit!

• • •

122. Myron, the hack, arrived at the golf club for his usual Saturday morning game. He was assigned a caddie, and seven hours later headed back to the clubhouse, complaining about his game and the poor advice his caddie gave him.

Frustrated beyond all belief, the caddie snapped back, "Gee, mister, it's too damn bad your IQ isn't as high as your golf score. That way you might be a physicist and be able to calculate your shots better!"

• • •

123. A hack golfer was at his usual one afternoon, chewing up sod and blaming the caddie, who was ready to quit. At one point the hack ripped up a sizable piece of turf and went ballistic. "What the hell am I supposed to do with this?" he screamed at the caddie.

"I suppose you could grow vegetables on it and feed a third-world country!" snapped the caddie.

• • •

124. Two guys show up for a round of golf one morning. One of them is dressed in all new golf attire.

First golfer: "Say, what do you think of my new golf duds?"

Second golfer: "Very nice, indeed."

First golfer: "There's still something missing, though. I can't put my finger on it."

Second golfer: "The way you golf, how about a pair of waders?!"

• • •

125. A guy was having trouble with his golf game. He tried everything but nothing worked. Finally he decided to spend big money and hire the best professional tutor he could find. They were out on the course the first day playing a round of golf. The pro took notes with every swing the golfer took. After the round the pro told the golfer to shower and change, and meet him in the clubhouse.

"Well, what do you suggest that I do to fix my game?" the golfer asked.

The pro thought for a moment. "First, I'd like you to sell your clubs, balls, and gadgets. Second, I'd like you to find a tree branch about the same size as your club, and find a bunch of rocks about the size of golf balls."

"Do you think that will help?"

"The way you golf, it couldn't hurt!"

• • •

126. Two rival golfers met up in the locker room after a round of golf. "Hey, Smedley, what did you shoot today?" the first one asked sarcastically.

"I shot a seventy-two, not that it's any of your business," Smedley sniped.

"Yeah, what'd you get on the back nine?"

• • •

127. A local amateur golfer was paired up with a touring pro in his club's annual pro-am tournament. At the end of the round the amateur was proud of the way he played and said to the pro, "We did pretty well today. What did you think of my game?"

"Not bad for your first time out!"

• • •

128. The hack golfer was taking his usual four hours just to play the front nine, and the caddie was getting more frustrated by the minute thinking of all the money he was losing.

"You must be tired of carrying that bag," said the golfer, apologetically.

"No, just tired of counting. I've had math tests easier than this!"

• • •

129. A guy arrived at the local club to play a round with some friends. He had on a new outfit and new shoes and had just bought new clubs. After the round he was complaining about his poor play. "I don't get it," he moaned. "I just spent a whole paycheck on new clubs and new accessories. I should be playing better than this."

His caddie quipped, "It's obvious you've been spending money on all the wrong things!"

• • •

130. A hack golfer and his friend had just completed a round of golf. The hacker, known for being hard on caddies, asked his friend, "What should I give the caddie?"

"How about your clubs?"

• • •

131. This golfer was so bad at tee shots that when he hit the ball and checked the ball marker, it read, "Just hit the damn ball already!"

• • •

132. Two competitive golfers finished the eighteenth and were headed for the clubhouse. The first one said, "It's a good thing for you I was off today."

"Off?" said the second. "Your game was so bad that if it had been a prizefight they would have stopped it after twelve holes!"

• • •

133. A hack golfer hated by all the caddies showed up one morning for a round of golf. This guy not only couldn't golf but complained about it all the time as well. All day long the guy kept saying, "Man, if I could only hit it as far as the pros, I could be so much better."

By the sixteenth hole the caddie was sick and tired of listening to this. Finally, he snapped and said, "Mister, if you could hit it as far as the pros, it would only mean you could hit that much further into the rough!"

• • •

134. A caddie had had all the abuse he could take for one day from the hack golfer. Hole after hole the golfer cursed and called him names. Finally, the golfer said, "You've got to be the stupidest caddie on earth!"

The caddie, not able to contain himself anymore, said, "You think I'm stupid? The next time my doctor tells me to work out with dumbbells, I'll just go for a walk with you!"

• • •

135. A husband and wife on vacation in Florida decided to visit the local country club for a round of golf. The husband rented clubs for himself and his wife, but the pro shop had only one bag. The wife insisted that the husband go out and play. He was paired with another gentleman.

After finishing the seventh hole the husband looked curiously across the green to see his wife and another woman teeing off on the fourth hole.

"Everything all right?" the second guy asked.

"Oh, sure," said the husband. "It seems my wife found an old bag to play with."

The guy looked over at the women. "Yeah, mine, too."

• • •

6

LIARS AND CHEATS

136. A golfer decides to invite two friends to golf with him and his regular partner. The four are enjoying a pleasant round and getting to know each other a little bit. They discuss different courses they've played, best tee shots, best putts, and the best round each guy has had. Every time a new question is asked, one of the regular golfers reaches into his pocket, pulls out an index card, and then gives his answer.

After the round, while having a few beers at the clubhouse, one of the new golfers quietly asks, "How come your friend always looks at an index card before giving an answer?"

"Oh, that," he said. "It's the only way he can remember what he's been telling people!"

• • •

137. An older guy was playing golf with his regular foursome when two young lads came up and asked if they could play through. The older guy became annoyed and said, "What's with you kids today? Why are you in such a hurry? I take my time and enjoy the game as well as everything around me. Besides, when I take my time, my score is the same as my age."

One of the young lads said, "Gee, you don't look 140!"

• • •

138. A father and young son came home from the golf course and were greeted at the door by the man's wife. "So how did you two do today?" she asked.

"Great," said the man. "I hit the woods perfectly today."

"Yeah," said the son innocently, "now all you have to do is learn how to hit out of them."

• • •

139. Two golfers were changing in the locker room after a round of golf and struck up a conversation. "So, how was your game today?" asked the first guy.

"Not bad, considering," said the second guy. "I can't complain. Besides—who'd listen? So, how about you?"

"Lousy," he said. "The only good thing to happen to me today was the birdie I got on the par sixteen on the eighteenth hole."

"What are you talking about?" asked the second guy. "There's no par-sixteen hole anywhere on this course."

"There is now," said the guy. "I own the course!"

• • •

140. Some buddies were sitting in the clubhouse enjoying some beers after a round of golf when the subject of "which club is best" came up.

"Well, I've played the game for more than forty years, and I have to vote for the five-wood," said one old duffer. "It's gotten me out of more bad situations than I care to admit."

"Nope. It's the three-wood that works the best, especially if your drives aren't as good as they should be," said another.

"You're both crazy!" exclaimed a third guy. "The best wood for getting out of serious trouble doesn't even go in your bag."

"Oh? What wood is that?" asked the first guy.

"My pencil!"

• • •

141. A really good golfer moved to town and decided to join the posh country club a few blocks away. He paid his dues and lit out for his first experience on the club's finest course. He specifically asked the club pro to be paired up with another good golfer so he could enjoy a competitive match. As it turned out, another newer member had also asked to be paired with a good golfer. "Is this guy *really* good?" asked the first golfer.

"Oh yes," said the pro. "He says he has a three handicap."

"Fine, I'll take him."

The two golfers and their caddies met at the first hole to tee off. By the ninth hole the first golfer was on par, while the second golfer was considerably below par, chewing grass as he played. While the second guy was looking for yet another lost ball, the first golfer looked at the caddies and said, "Say, I thought the club pro said this guy had a three handicap. What gives?"

"Him?" Both caddies laughed. "He means per hole!"

• • •

142. Two guys just finished the eleventh hole at Pebble Beach when one asked, "Say, what did you get on this hole?"

"Who, me?" said the second golfer. "Oh, I got a five."

"Five!" exclaimed the first golfer. "Who are you trying to kid? You took five just getting to the green!"

"Fine," said the second angrily. "You want to get technical? Make it nine!"

• • •

143. Two friends had been playing a round of golf every Saturday for a few years with one golfer always winning. One particular Saturday the match was closer than usual. In fact, it was tied when they came to the eighteenth. Try as he might, the losing golfer couldn't seem to pull out a victory, and started swearing and throwing his clubs.

"Hey, calm down," said the winning golfer. "You played a great game and had me worried right up to the end."

"That's why I'm so angry," said the losing golfer. "I cheated like crazy and *still* couldn't win!"

• • •

144. A foursome arrived at the long par-3 thirteenth hole to tee off. The green for this hole was hidden by a huge bunker, so there was no way to tell where a shot landed until the golfer arrived at the green.

After the last player hit his shot, the first guy ran off down the fairway without waiting for the others. He disappeared behind the bunker and seconds later came running back, screaming, "I got a hole in one! Incredible! Never in my life! I got a hole in one!"

"Who are you trying to kid?" said one of the golfers. "You ran up ahead of us and had plenty of time to put your ball in the cup. How in the world can you expect us to believe you?"

"I swear to God it's true," he insisted, crossing his heart. "If you don't believe me, go check the cup. I left the ball in there to prove it!"

• • •

145. Golf has made more liars out of Americans than all of the income tax forms ever filed.

• • •

146. Contrary to popular belief, avid golfers do not lie all the time. Anytime one golfer calls another a liar he's probably telling the truth.

• • •

147. First golfer: "So how's your golf game these days?"
Second golfer: "I'm a keep and scratch golfer."
First golfer: "What the heck is that?"
Second golfer: "I keep the scores I like and scratch the ones I don't."

• • •

148. Two friends were talking in the clubhouse over drinks one day about golfing buddies they knew. "When it comes to luck, that guy Jim is the luckiest guy on earth," said the first.

"What makes you say that?" asked the second.

"Every time he hits his ball into the rough, he wanders out to find it, and without fail, he always finds it sitting directly on top of someone else's lost tee!"

• • •

149. Two hack golfers meet up in the clubhouse after a round of golf. One comes up to the other and says, "Drinks are on me! I just shot the game of a lifetime—a seventy-eight!"

"A seventy-eight?" says the second guy. "How the heck did you do that? Next to me, you're the worst putter in history!"

"I got a new club that changed all that," explains the first. "You know the course rule that says if your ball is within a club's length of the hole, it's a gimme?"

"Yeah, what about it?" asks the second.

The guy reaches into his bag, gets his ball retriever, and opens it to its full extension of twenty feet.

"Don't you know what this is?" asks the second guy, laughing.

"I sure do," responds the first guy confidently. "The guy who sold it to me called it a water club!"

• • •

150. Four college seniors decided to drive to a posh golf resort for a weekend of golf and partying instead of studying for the big final exam in calculus on Monday. Each had a good grade going into the exam, so they figured they would just cram on Sunday night. As it turned out, they met some beautiful women at the resort and golfed and partied with them until Sunday midnight. While driving back, they all agreed that they would tell the professor that while driving home they had a blowout and didn't have a spare, and they would beg to take the exam late.

Well, their little scheme worked. When they showed up for the makeup exam on Tuesday, the professor was there with four exam booklets. He led each to a separate room, handed him a book, and told him he had two hours to complete the test. The first question, worth five points, had to do with the chain rule as applied to limits. An easy question. Each felt at ease, thinking the whole test would be a cinch.

The second question, worth ninety-five points: Which tire?

• • •

151. Two guys had been planning a big golf outing for weeks. They both had the day off and new equipment to try. The first guy, a bachelor, arrived at his friend's house at seven A.M. to drive him to the course.

"Bye, honey, we'll be back by noon," shouted the other golfer.

"I thought we were going to play thirty-six holes. What do you mean by telling her we'll be back by noon?" asked the friend on the way to the car.

"I didn't say which day!"

• • •

152. A foursome was getting tanked one Saturday afternoon after a fun round of golf. They started discussing great golf courses and how the game was invented. One fellow spoke up, "You know, it's a well-known fact that Samson was the world's first golf addict."

"Aw, you're nuts," retorted another golfer. "What makes you think Samson was the first golf addict?"

"Think about it. Even with all his mighty strength he couldn't break away from the links!"

• • •

153. First golfer: "Hey, I don't like the way you cheat all the time when we golf."

Second golfer: "If you've got a better way, I'm open to suggestions!"

• • •

154. Four buddies had been golfing together for ten years. For the whole time three of the buddies suspected the fourth of cheating on his shots and scorecard but could never prove it. It became a contest to see who could catch him. One day the group was teeing off on the twelfth hole at their club. This particular hole had a deep ravine that required a 165-yard carry to clear. Three of the buddies came up just short of the ravine, but the fourth guy went over the edge and disappeared. He went down into the ravine to play his second shot while his buddies waited for him on the other side. A few minutes later the guy's ball came rolling down the fairway.

"How many shots did it take to get out?" asked one of the three.

"Oh, I got out in one," said the fourth.

"What are you talking about?" said another of the three. "We distinctly heard you take five swings at the ball!"

"Um, er, that's just the echoes from the ravine being so deep," the fourth stammered nervously.

"Aha!" screamed another of the three. "We finally caught you! How do you explain the five different cuss words heard after each echo?"

• • •

155. A guy came home from golfing and was eerily quiet at the dinner table. "You've hardly spoken two words since you came home," said his wife. "What's wrong?"

"What's wrong? I'll tell you what's wrong," he ranted. "That SOB golfing partner of mine is the biggest cheater on earth. We were tied going into the eighteenth. We both hit our fairway shots toward the green and went to find them. After a couple of minutes he screamed out that he'd found his and that it was about two feet from the cup. I knew he was lying because I had his ball in my pocket the whole time!"

• • •

156. A guy came home from his club and began crying the minute he came through the door.
"What's the matter with you?" asked his wife.
"We were discussing scores at the clubhouse and I told the truth. They revoked my membership!"

• • •

157. A shrink and his patient decided to play a round of golf. The patient said, "I'm going to use a special ball that's guaranteed to make me a winner today." He reached into his golf bag and pretended to pull out a golf ball. The psychiatrist decided to go along with it. Going to the eighteenth hole, the patient, not surprisingly, had a one-stroke lead. The shrink, being fairly competitive, announced to his patient that he, too, would be using a special ball, and proceeded to pull out an invisible ball from his golf bag.
The patient swung hard and said, "Wow, a perfect shot, 280 yards away!"
The shrink teed up and swung hard. "Excellent shot, 275 yards away!"
They walked up to the fairway and the shrink set up for his next shot. "Holy mackerel! It looks like it's going in the cup . . . and yes! I win the match!"
"Hold on," said the patient. "You're disqualified."
"What do you mean I'm disqualified?" said the shrink.
"You hit the wrong ball!"

• • •

158. Two old golfing buddies happened to meet at the local watering hole and started discussing their golf games. "Say, have you tried that new municipal course in the next county?" asked the first guy. "I tried it yesterday."

"So did I," said the second guy, surprised.

"Oh yeah? What'd you shoot on the first hole?" asked the first guy.

"Five," said the second guy.

"I shot a four," said the first guy, taking a drink of beer. "What'd you get on the second?"

"I shot a four," said the second guy. "What did you get?"

"I shot a perfect three," said the first guy. "How'd you do on the third?"

"Bad. I got a six," said the second guy. "And you?"

"Oh, I got a four," said the first guy. "What was your score on the fourth hole?"

"Oh no," said the second guy, suspiciously, "This time *you* go first!"

• • •

ONE-LINERS, ETC.

159. Q: What do you call a blonde golfer with an IQ of 125?
A: A foursome.

• • •

160. Bumper Sticker: Old golfers never die. . . . They just can't find their balls like they used to!

• • •

161. Two golfers are getting set for their tee shots at the fourth hole. The first golfer says, "Hey, guess what?! I got a set of golf clubs for my wife!"
The second golfer replies, "Great trade!"

• • •

162. Q: Why do golfers wear two pairs of pants?
A: In case they get a hole in one!

• • •

163. Q: Why do they call it golf?
A: All the good four-letter words were taken.

• • •

164. Q: What is the difference between a lost golf ball and the G-spot?
A: A man will spend five minutes looking for the lost golf ball.

• • •

165. A sign at the golf course detailing the dress code:
Guys: No Shirt, No Golf.
Girls: No Shirt, No Greens Fees.

• • •

166. Two golfers are on the seventeenth at Augusta. One says, "My wife says if I don't stop playing golf she's gonna leave me. Gee, thirty-five years of marriage down the drain!"

• • •

167. In primitive society, when native tribes beat the ground with clubs and yelled, it was called witchcraft. Today, it's called golf.

• • •

168. Q: What is a Michigan golfer's favorite winter wine?
A: I wanna go to Miami.

• • •

169. Golf is a game where the slowest people in the world are those in front of you and the fastest are those behind.

• • •

170. A bad golfer is one who addresses the ball twice: once before swinging, and once after swinging.

• • •

171. Many golfers prefer golf carts to caddies. Carts can't count, criticize, or laugh.

• • •

172. Q: How can you tell a bad golfer from a bad sky diver?
A: Bad golfer: Whack! Oh, *shit!* Bad skydiver: Oh, *shit!* Whack!

• • •

173. The other day I was playing golf and I hit two of my best balls. I stepped on a rake in the sand trap.

• • •

174. A wife was mad at her husband for forgetting their anniversary. "You think so much about your golf game that you don't even remember when we were married," she said.

"Of course I do, my dear. It was the day after I sank that thirty-foot putt at Pebble Beach."

• • •

175. What's the difference between golfing in New York and golfing in Canada?
In New York they say, "Eeehhh, get off da green!"
In Canada they say, "Get off da green, eeehhh."

• • •

176. During an important pro-am tournament a professional's partner asked, "Well, what do you think of my game?"
"It's okay," said the pro, "but I prefer golf!"

• • •

177. A golfer had made an awful shot and tore up a rather large piece of turf. He picked it up, looked at his caddie, and said, "What should I do with this?"
"If I were you," said the caddie, "I'd take it home to practice on."

• • •

178. A wife walked into the bedroom and found her husband in bed with his set of Ping golf clubs. Seeing the astonished look on her face, he calmly said, "Well, you said I had to choose, right?"

• • •

179. If you think it's hard to meet new people, try picking up the wrong golf ball on a golf course sometime.

• • •

180. Two old golfing buddies were standing in the pouring rain getting ready to hit their shots near a river where two guys were fishing. One golfer looked to the other and said, "Look at those idiots fishing in the rain."

• • •

181. Q: Why are golf and sex so similar?
A: Neither is much fun if you have to count strokes.

• • •

182. I once played a course that was so tough, I lost two balls in the ball washer!

• • •

183. Q. What is the only iron that can come between a golfer and his clubs?

A. A skillet!

• • •

184. Q. Why are there eighteen holes on a golf course?

A. Because that's how long it took the Scots who invented the game to finish a bottle of whiskey!

• • •

185. A bunch of friends were in the locker room changing after a round of golf. One guy looked puzzled at his friend and said, "Say, how long have you been wearing a garter belt?"

"Ever since my wife found it in the backseat of the car."

• • •

186. Student: "Let me get this straight. The less I hit the ball, the better I am doing."

Pro: "Now you've got it!"

Student: "Then why hit it at all?"

• • •

187. In golf, you drive for show and putt for dough.

• • •

188. The hack golfer noticed his caddie looking at his watch every five minutes. "Caddie, why do you keep looking at your watch?" asked the angered golfer.

"It's not a watch," replied the caddie. "It's a compass."

• • •

189. Two golfers were sitting in the clubhouse commiserating on how badly they golfed throughout the year when one said to the other, "Oh yeah, well, my game was so bad this year I had to have my ball retriever regripped."

• • •

190. Old duffer: "What a day. I've never played this badly before!"

Caddie: "Really? I didn't realize you had played before!"

• • •

191. Hack golfer: "Say, caddie. Do you think my game is improving?"

Caddie: "Why, yes. You're missing the ball much less than you used to!"

• • •

192. Golfer no. 1: "My wife says if I don't stop playing golf so much she's going to leave me!"

Golfer no. 2: "Don't worry. After two or three days you won't even miss her."

• • •

193. Hack golfer: "Say, caddie, do you think it is a sin to play golf on Sunday?"

Caddie: "The way you play, it's a crime any day of the week!"

• • •

194. There are three ways to improve your golf game: take lessons, practice constantly, or learn to cheat.

• • •

195. I once knew a golfer who cheated so much when he got a hole in one he wrote down zero!

• • •

196. You haven't really played golf until you've had to decide which opening in the trees gives you the best chance of getting back to the fairway.

• • •

197. Golf is what men play when they're too big for marbles.

• • •

198. The man who invented golf and said it was enjoyable is the same man who invented bagpipes and said it was music!

• • •

199. Q. What's the difference between a pro golfer and God?
A. God doesn't think He's a golfer.

• • •

200. Definition of a fairway: An unfamiliar and unforgiving tract of closely cropped grass running directly from the tee to the green. Balls can usually be found to the immediate left or right of it.

• • •

201. A wise man once said the quickest and easiest way to lower your golf score is with an eraser!

• • •

202. You know you're a real hack when your divot flies farther than your ball!

• • •

203. A frugal man enjoys shooting in the 130s, figuring he's getting more for his money.

• • •

204. The only difference between a blown shot and a practice swing is that nobody curses for five minutes after a practice swing.

• • •

205. Why is it that some men can't add when it comes to the family budget but turn into mathematicians on the golf course?

• • •

206. Two golfers were playing a quick round when they came upon an older couple. "Hey, buddy, why don't you help your wife find her ball so we can play through?"
"Oh, she found her ball. Now she's looking for her club."

• • •

207. A hack golfer comes home from the course and is greeted by his wife, who asks, "How'd you golf today, dear?"
"Well, I didn't win, but I got a lot of practice. I got to hit the ball more than anyone else!"

• • •

208. A guy calls his family doctor in a panic. "Doctor, doctor, I've got an emergency! My baby son just swallowed all my golf tees. What should I do?"
"Practice your putting until I get there!"

• • •

209. Q: Why do white men play golf?
A: So they can dress like pimps!

• • •

210. It seems the older I get, the longer the fairways and the smaller the holes get.

• • •

211. Golf and sex are just about the only things you can enjoy without being good at them.

• • •

212. He's such a bad golfer that, when he comes to play, the rangers fly the flags on the greens at half-staff.

• • •

213. When a golfer goes golfing with his boss, he should never shoot below ninety. If he shoots higher than ninety, his boss

won't ask him to play anymore. If he shoots lower, the boss will know he's been ducking work and fire him.

• • •

214. He's such a bad golfer, if he grew tomatoes they'd come up sliced.

• • •

215. Caddie to his golfer: "Look, I'm not saying you're a bad golfer, but why don't you take two or three weeks off and then quit all together!"

• • •

216. A true sportsman never picks up lost golf balls while they're still rolling.

• • •

217. This guy is so obsessed with golf he thinks the Green Party is a division of the Golfers Association.

• • •

218. My game is so bad that warning sirens go off in three counties when I tee up.

• • •

219. Q: Why is playing golf like paying taxes?
    A: Because no matter how hard you drive for the green, you still end up in the hole.

• • •

220. First golfer: "Hey, how's your golf game?"
    Second golfer: "Not so good. It seems the older I get, the better I used to be!"

• • •

221. A professional golfer was talking to some friends about his bad year. "My golf game was so bad this year that I received get-well cards from four credit card companies and the IRS."

• • •

222. Heard the one about the woman who was nervous about dinner? Her husband was out shooting golf and she didn't know how to prepare them. (Good thing he doesn't shoot craps!)

• • •

223. A "handicapped golfer" is a man who plays golf with his wife.

• • •

224. My son is so good at golf he's been offered a full scholarship to medical school.

• • •

225. A dim-witted golfer in a foreign country was sentenced to be hanged and he asked the warden if he could take a few practice swings first.

• • •

226. Golf is the best sport. Husbands can spend the entire weekend with a bunch of hookers and their wives don't care.

• • •

227. Proof that golfers are self-abusive: Who else would spend that much time and effort on a game that spelled backwards reads *flog*?

• • •

228. The best tip you give is the one you give the starter!

• • •

229. First golfer: "Don't your kids mind that you spend every Sunday afternoon playing golf instead of playing with them?"

Second golfer: "Oh, heck no. The way I play, in three more Sundays I will have filled the sandbox!"

• • •

230. Overheard at a golf gadget inventors convention: Someone should invent a ball that curses violently when you lose it. This will save a lot of embarrassment for those golfers who get thrown out of their golf clubs!

• • •

231. First golfer: "You can always tell how good a golf course is by church attendance."
Second golfer: "Oh yeah? How's that?"
First golfer: "The better the course, the fewer the people who attend church."

• • •

232. Q: Why are blondes so eager to take up golf?
A: They heard there were diamonds in the rough!

• • •

233. Golfer's Hope: Hitting an excellent shot your first time out and playing for thirty years thinking you'll actually do it again.

• • •

234. A guy lived a half mile from the local course and liked to play as often as possible. One day he went into the pro shop and bought a dozen balls. "You want these wrapped?" asked the clerk.
"No, thanks," said the man, "I'll just drive them home."

• • •

235. Whether a ball is actually lost or has just been hit improperly is merely a difference of opinion.

• • •

236. I knew a golfer who was so bad he couldn't hit his mulligan!

• • •

237. Mulligan: Dé jà pu! (Or, proof that lightning does strike in the same place twice!)

• • •

238. Bumper sticker: Old golfers never die. . . . They just lose distance.

• • •

239. When the golf pro told his student she was only average, he was being mean!

• • •

240. Golfer: "Oh, look, that's my evil mother-in-law up there on the clubhouse patio watching us. Let's see if I can make this shot."

Partner: "You'll never hit her with that club. Here, try my Big Bertha!"

• • •

241. There was a big, big man at the golf club who could hit the ball so hard and so far that they erected a special ball marker with his name on it that said YOU DA MAN!

• • •

242. The difference between learning to golf and learning to drive is that with golf you hit everything and with cars you hit nothing. Unfortunately, some people often get confused as to which one they're doing at any given time!

• • •

243. Q: How can you tell which of two golfers is the boss and which is the employee?

A: The employee is the one who says "Oops!" after hitting a hole in one.

• • •

244. By the time you pay for new clubs, new clothes, accessories, a round of golf, and a cart, it doesn't take long to realize that the clubs aren't the only things getting shafted!

• • •

245. It's widely accepted in the golf world that professional golfers have every right to make more money than the president—they hit fewer people when they play.

• • •

246. Hacker: With my score today I'll never be able to hold my head up.

Caddie: Why not? You've been doing it all afternoon.

• • •

247. Golfer: You perhaps won't believe it, but I once did this hole in one.

Caddie: Would that be one stroke or one day, sir?

• • •

248. Hacker: Any ideas on how I can cut about ten strokes off my score?
Caddie: Yes, quite on nine.

• • •

249. Gimme: An agreement between two losers who can't putt.

• • •

250. Q. What are the four worst words you could hear during a game in golf?
A. It's still your turn!

• • •

251. Q. Which is the easiest golf stroke?
A. The fourth putt!

• • •

252. Q. You're putting out on a long par-3. Where's the safest place to be when the group behind you is starting to tee off?
A. Right near the hole!

• • •

253. Funny thing about golf and polo: Both have lots of fertilizer, but one uses a horse to spread it!

• • •

254. Ever wonder what professional golfers do after they retire?

• • •

255. Q: What's the last thing a stripper takes off in Florida?
A: Her golf shoes.

• • •

256. Q: What do you call a rich woman who shanks all her shots?
A: A high-class hooker.

• • •

257. Two golfers were out playing one morning. One wasn't doing so hot and said, "First it was my marriage; now, the magic has gone out of my nine-iron, too."

• • •

258. Men are strange: They'll gladly walk thirty-six holes of golf but won't get up to get a beer at home.

• • •

259. A recent survey showed that many men are claiming that golf has replaced sex as the American sport. Of course, over 70 percent of the men polled were over sixty-five.

• • •

260. If you can keep a smile on your face throughout the whole game while others curse and lose their heads . . . you must be the caddie.

• • •

GOLF NUTS

261. Several members at the local country club complained about the behavior of Bob, one of the newest members. It seems he was always making crazy bets with other members. It wasn't the betting that offended everyone, it was the oddity of the bets and his weird behavior. Bob had just picked out his caddie and was headed for the course when the pro decided to follow along and investigate. The pro met up with him at the second hole and asked if he could join him to see for himself. On the third hole Bob said, "If you make this putt, I'll bite my eyeball."

The pro looked at him and said, "Either you're nuts or you've been drinking too much. I'm afraid I'll have to ask you to leave."

Bob laughed and said, "Wait, I'll bet you fifty bucks on top of it."

The pro only had a six-foot putt, so he decided to take the bet. "Fine, I'll take your bet, but if you fail to pay up in full, you'll pay me double and agree to leave." The pro sank his putt and collected fifty dollars. "Wait a minute," said the pro. "What about your eye?"

Joe removed a glass eye and started biting it. The pro was upset at being had, but decided to get Bob on the next hole. The pro ended up hitting his ball into a sand trap, thirty-five feet from the green. Bob walked up to him and said, "Hit it on the green from here and I'll bite my other eye."

Well, the pro knew there was no way in heck Bob could have two glass eyes. He said, "Fine. You got a bet, but it will cost you another fifty dollars. If you fail to pay, you'll owe me triple."

The pro hit the ball on the green, twelve feet from the cup, and collected another fifty dollars.

"So, what about the eye thing?" asked the pro. Bob removed his false teeth and bit his other eye.

The pro was furious and couldn't wait for Bob to slip up. Sure enough, on the next hole, Bob made another offer. The pro's green shot had an uphill lie about fifteen feet from the cup. Bob said, "Make that putt and I'll urinate into the cup from the cart."

Now, the cart was a good twenty-five yards away and the pro knew for sure he had him this time. "You'll do it from where the cart is now?" asked the pro.

"With my eyes closed," said Bob. "And not miss with one drop. Plus, I'll even double the bet."

The pro smiled. "You got yourself a bet." The pro concentrated for a moment and sank a perfect putt. Bob handed him one hundred dollars, walked over to the cart, and got ready to pay off the rest of his bet. Bob urinated all over the green and on the fairway, but didn't come even remotely close to the cup. Smiling, he handed the pro another hundred dollars. As Bob walked away the pro asked him, "Why did you make such a crazy bet? Now you're out one hundred dollars."

Bob smiled at the pro and said, "Really? I bet my caddie a thousand dollars I could urinate on your green and you wouldn't get mad!"

• • •

262. Four international business executives are grouped together for a round of golf at Hilton Head. At the fourth tee a funny ringing sound is heard. The British golfer goes to his golf bag, pulls out his cellular phone, and has a brief conversation with his firm.

"I say, terribly sorry, old chaps, but one has to keep one's finger on the pulse and all that rot." The rest of the group nods understandingly.

On the sixth tee there's another funny ring, but not from the golf bag. The American says, "Y'all are gonna have to excuse me a minute." The man places his thumb to his ear and holds his pinkie near his mouth and has an intense conversation with his partner. He turns back to the group and says, "Oh, this is the latest thing in Texas. I've had a microphone implanted in my pinkie and a receiver implanted in my thumb. It's downright convenient!"

Play goes on for a few more holes, at which point there is a strange-sounding ringing noise. The Frenchman, who had been setting up his putt, snaps to attention, turns to the east, and says, "Oui, oui, je comprend. Oui. Au revoir." He looks back to the group to see them all staring at him.

"Ah, this iz really state of ze art, no?" he says. "I have ze microphone grafted into mah lower lip, and ze receiver grafted into my earlobe. All I have to do iz straighten my neck to answer ze phone." The group is obviously impressed.

Then, on the eighteenth hole, quiet "bing-bongs" are heard. There's no one left but the guy from Japan, so they all turn to look at him. The Japanese businessman lays down his putter, mutters "so sorry," bows, and runs into some nearby bushes. The group passes the time by discussing international business laws and their luck dating foreign women. After about ten minutes the American goes to the bushes to check on the man from Japan. He's astonished to find him squatting and grimacing, with his pants down and his eyes closed. "Hey, buddy, you okay?" he asks.

"Oh yes, please. Everything is fine. Just awaiting fax from home office."

• • •

263. Four golfers playing a serious match approached the eleventh green. All of a sudden one guy fell down and the other three started fighting. The course ranger saw this and

drove up to them to stop the fight and find out what was going on. "What the heck are you guys doing and why is this man on the ground?" he asked.

One guy spoke up, "My friend here just had a stroke and these two idiots want to include it on the scorecard!"

• • •

264. A Scotsman and an American were paired up for a match at St. Andrews one Sunday by the club pro. They started talking about playing golf during the various seasons of the year. "You know, in most parts of the States we can't play in the wintertime. We have to wait until spring," said the American.

"Why, in Scotland we even play in the wintertime. Snow and cold don't bother us real golfers," said the Scot.

"What do you do? Paint your balls black?" asked the American.

"No," said the Scot. "We just put on an extra sweater or two."

• • •

265. An avid golfer's marriage started to have serious problems as he was playing golf five days a week. He and his wife talked about it after dinner one night. "I have an idea. Why don't you teach me how to play golf? This way we can golf once or twice a week together and work on our marriage at the same time," she said.

He argued that golf is a serious game for serious people and that she was just trying to prove her point by making a mockery of the game. After several hours of debate, he could see he was getting nowhere and reluctantly agreed.

The next day they went to the course to sign her up for lessons with the local pro. The lessons were five days a week, and he was happy that she was no longer bothering him. One day, one of his buddies asked him how things were working out.

"It's great, actually," he said. "Ever since she signed up for lessons, she doesn't bother me and lets me play all the golf I want."

His buddy replied, "Well, I guess I should tell you that she's having a wild affair with the golf pro."

The man became furious. His eyes turned red and he bent his driver over his knee. "I knew it wouldn't last. I knew she'd make a mockery of the game!"

• • •

266. A father sat down to have a heart-to-heart with his oldest son. "Son," he said, "it's time we had a little talk. I'm sure you know what I'm referring to. You're getting older now, and soon you'll have urges and feelings you've never had before. Your heart will pound, your hands will sweat, and you'll go through mood swings. You'll be totally preoccupied and won't be able to think of anything else. I don't want you to worry. It's perfectly normal. . . . It's called golf."

• • •

267. Two men met up for their usual round of golf one Saturday morning. The first guy said, "Say, what do you think of the new club pro? I hear he's pretty good."

"I'm not sure I care for him much," remarked the second guy. "I think he's a little strange."

"Oh, how so?" asked the first guy.

"The other day he came up to me and started to correct my stance without asking."

"What's odd about that? He's just trying to help your game," said the first guy.

"I was standing at the urinal at the time."

• • •

268. An avid golfer was sailing on his boat one day when a freak storm came up suddenly putting him way off course and marooning him on an island. Some months later a cruise liner spotted the man swinging at something and decided to investigate. The captain and a landing party were amazed to discover that this fellow had cleared away enough island brush to build a crude nine-hole golf course. The guy used driftwood for drivers, whale bones for irons, coral for a putter, and golf balls carved from pumice stones.

"This is impressive," said the captain. "You must be quite proud of yourself."

"Well," said the man, "the greens aren't much to look at, but I am quite proud of the water hazard."

• • •

269. A scratch golfer decided to play a few rounds of golf to practice up for a big tournament on the following weekend. The weather turned bad as he arrived at the course, but the golfer decided to play anyway. Try as he might, the normally good golfer was having a lousy game. On the first hole it started to sprinkle—he hit par. On the third hole it started to hail—he was one over par. On the sixth hole it was a torrential downpour—he lost two balls. And, on the eleventh hole, his bag was struck by lightning and burned to a crisp.

At this the golfer bent his club over his knee, hurled it into the rough, and screamed at the heavens, "Why don't you come down here and fight fair!"

• • •

270. For two long years a team of top archeologists from around the world had been toiling away deep in a jungle, carefully clearing away brush, trees, and overgrowth that covered a lost city. Their excitement grew as the city's real purpose became more and more clear. From the long narrow lanes of giant flagstones and the perfectly circular holes every few hundred yards or so, it was obvious that it was an ancient golf course. Stone panels with carved images showed human figures using primitive prototypes of modern clubs and putters. The team decided to consult with the chief of the local tribe regarding traditions surrounding prehistoric golf. The chief said that, in fact, the original people did play a form of golf at the site until tragedy struck. The top archeologist spoke up and asked, "What kind of tragedy could have stopped them from ever playing golf at such a beautiful spot?"

"It's obvious," said the chief pointing to the overgrowth. "They couldn't afford the greens fees."

• • •

271. Two old friends bumped into each other at the supermarket one day. They discussed little things like work and kids, when one said, "Everything is great, except I haven't seen my husband in ten years."

"Oh, I'm sorry to hear that," said the other one. "Divorce? Death?"

"Golf." said the first.

• • •

272. A professional female golfer had to leave the ladies tour when she became pregnant. Not wanting to lose her golfing skills, she begged the doctor to let her continue to play golf during the pregnancy, to which he agreed. She came home after a quick round one day and her husband asked, "So, how did it go?"

"Excellent," she said. "So much so that I swear I could hear the baby applauding when I birdied the fourteenth!"

• • •

273. A man decided to take up golf so he could spend more time with his clients and friends. After ten years of him virtually never being home, the man's wife said, "You love that damn golf game more than you love me! I swear, if you ever stayed home on a Sunday, I'd have a stroke and drop dead!"

The man smiled and said, "You'd do that for me?"

• • •

274. An avid golfer was shooting a practice round before going to the country club over the weekend to try and qualify for the pro circuit. He hit his tee shot on the seventh hole, a long par-4 with a slight dogleg left, which landed on the fairway about 190 yards away. "What do you suggest for this lie?" he asked the caddie.

"Well," said the caddie, "last week we had a few pros out here practicing. One of the pros had about the same lie as you do. Now, what I told him was . . ."

The impatient golfer cut him off, saying, "Skip the dissertation, kid. Just give me the club the pro used."

"But wait," started the caddie.

"Wait nothing, kid. Just give me the club!" snapped the golfer.

The guy approached the ball, took his swing, and watched the ball land in the fairway a good twenty-five yards short of the green.

"What the heck are you trying to do to me, kid? I'm not even close to the green," said the angry golfer.

"That's what I tried to tell you. Neither was the pro."

• • •

275. An avid golfer hit his tee shot on the first hole 300 yards right down the middle of the fairway. When the ball came down, however, it bounced off a sprinkler head and headed into some trees. The angry golfer went into the trees, found his ball, and hit a very hard 2-iron. The ball struck a tree and bounced straight back at him. It nailed him in the temple and killed him instantly. The man was at the Pearly

Gates; St. Peter looked at the Big Book and said, "Hmm. I see you were a golfer, is that correct?"

"Yes, sir," he replied.

"We have some pretty good courses up here. Are you any good?" asked St. Peter.

"Am I any good!" beamed the man. "I got *here* in two, didn't I?"

• • •

276. A golfer went to the clubhouse after his weekly round of golf to have a few beers with his friends. "You know, I think that guy in the blue shirt in the group behind us is crazy," said the golfer.

"Why do you say that?" asked another golfer. "Did he cuss, throw his clubs, chew up turf? What?"

"No, none of that," said the golfer. "This guy kept score in ink!"

• • •

277. A man and woman are set to be married in one week. The church and hall are reserved, flower arrangements and bouquets have been ordered, and the band and caterer are booked. The bride and bridesmaids have attended to every little detail. This is going to be the perfect wedding. Then the bride-to-be gets a frantic phone call from her fiancé.

"We can't get married next week," he exclaims excitedly. "It just won't work. We need to postpone it for a day or two."

"What, are you nuts?" shouts the woman. "Everything's set. We can't change the date now. What could be more important than this, anyway?"

"Well," says the man sheepishly, "according to the calendar, our twenty-fifth wedding anniversary would fall on a Sunday, and you know I never miss golf on Sunday!"

• • •

278. Two avid golfers were golfing on the back nine one afternoon. The first guy was enjoying a decent round, while the second was ripping up the course and complaining about it all afternoon.

"That's it!" he screamed after missing yet another easy putt. "I can't take it anymore. I'm supposed to be relaxing out here, and I'm more stressed than ever. I need to take a vacation."

"But isn't a vacation supposed to be where you go away and play golf? Where are you going to go to get away from it?" asked the second guy.

"I know, I'll spend some time at the office!"

• • •

279. A man came home to eat after playing thirty-six holes at the local municipal course. He was two hours late and his wife was fuming. "Thanks to you, another dinner is ruined!" she barked. "You spend way too much time at the golf course and not enough time with the family."

"That's funny," said the man. "My caddie today said the same thing. The kid looked familiar, too."

"That caddie was your son, you moron!"

• • •

280. Just after the turn of the century, golf was starting to catch on in the Old West. They had been playing it for years back East, and a few smart fellers decided to bring it West. Because it was so hot out there near the desert, the rich folk didn't want to walk when they played, so they had the local blacksmith convert an old mine car into sort of a prehistoric golf cart with a big surrey on it. There wasn't any way to power it back then, so they would hire Indians to push them around the course.

Well, one day, a bunch of rich swells who were out golfing decided to stop at the watering hole located between the ninth and tenth holes and cool off with a mug of beer or two. One of the fellers looked at the Indian and said, "Now, look, you. I don't like to sit in hot seats, and worse yet, I don't like to play with hot clubs. We're gonna be inside for a respite, so while we're gone, I want you to run around this cart and create a little breeze to keep everything cool." And with that he flipped the Indian a nickel.

About half an hour later a cowboy came in and said, "Hey, who owns this here fancy mine car with all the new-fangled golf stuff in it?"

"I do," said one of the rich fellers, standing up. "Why, what's wrong with it?"

"Nothing's wrong with it, mister, but you left your Injun runnin'."

• • •

281. Crazy Bob arrived at the club for a round of golf on Saturday. He got the name Crazy Bob because he was known to pull all kinds of crazy stunts that generally pissed everyone off. He got a tee time and a caddie and strolled out to the first tee. "Hand me my putter," said Bob.

"You can't use a putter to tee off," said the caddie. "It won't go anywhere."

"Just hand me the damn putter," said Bob.

The caddie handed Bob the putter and WHAM, somehow the ball went flying 225 yards. "Now hand me my pitching wedge," he said.

The caddie tried to put up an argument, but Bob waved him off and pointed to the pitching wedge. The caddie handed it to him and, sure enough, he landed on the green. "Now hand me my one-wood," said Bob.

The caddie thought he would never sink a fifteen-foot putt with a driver and protested, but he handed it to him nonetheless. With an effortless attempt, Crazy Bob sank the putt. Then Bob walked over to the cup and just stared down for what seemed to be an eternity.

"Something wrong, sir?" asked the caddie.

Bob looked at him blankly. "What club do I use to get it out?"

• • •

282. There was a golf fanatic who loved the game so much, he traveled practically all over the world visiting different courses. His bag was adorned with stickers and patches from many of the courses he had played, and he was quite

87

proud of the unique collection of golf balls he had accumulated from each course. Well, one day he was at a new course in the South, enjoying another good round of golf. On the thirteenth hole he noticed the course ranger and an older man driving toward him in a cart.

"Is this the guy?" said the ranger to the old man while pointing at the golfer.

"I'm not sure," said the old man. "It kind of looks like him, but I can't really tell."

"What's the problem?" asked the golfer, quizzically.

"What's the problem? I'll tell you the problem, boy," said the ranger. "Somebody is stealing other people's balls from the fairways, and I think it's you."

"That's crazy! I've never stolen anyone's ball," snapped the golfer.

"Oh yeah? Well, we'll see about that," said the ranger. "I've got the best sense of smell in the world, and can tell where any ball came from. Open up your ball bag."

The golfer sensed that this could be big trouble, so he quickly and obediently opened his bag. The ranger reached inside, pulled out a ball, and sniffed.

"Ha! This ball is from Pebble Beach. You got a receipt for this ball?"

The golfer pointed to a patch on his bag and said, "Played there last year."

The ranger frowned even harder, reached in for another ball, and sniffed it, saying, "This ball is from Hilton Head. You got a receipt for this one?"

The golfer turned his bag and pointed to another patch and said, "Played there two years ago."

The ranger got really mad, reached deep into the bag, and pulled out yet another ball, and sniffed. "This ball came from St. Andrews. Let's see your receipt for this one!" he said angrily.

The golfer pointed to another patch and said, "Honeymooned there with my wife in '91."

"You think you're pretty smart, don't ya, boy!" snarled the ranger. "Just where the hell are you from?"

By this point the golfer was pissed. He pulled down his pants and said, "Why don't you take a whiff and tell me."

• • •

283. There were three pieces of string that really wanted to play at an exclusive golf club. The first string entered the clubhouse and asked the pro, "How much to play nine holes?"

The pro pointed toward the door and said, "Get out of here! We don't allow strings on the golf course."

The string went back to his friends and told them what had happened. The second string got mad and charged into the clubhouse, saying, "I'm playing golf today. I've got plenty of money, so give me a cart."

"You don't fool me!" shouted the pro. "You're one of those strings, and we don't allow you in here."

The second string returned and told his friends what had happened. The third string, being the smartest of the three, tied himself into a knot and shredded both his ends. "Watch this, boys," he said, "I'm playing eighteen today."

With that, he walked into the club. "I'm playing eighteen today," he announced. The pro glared at him rather suspiciously and said, "Hey, you wouldn't be one of those strings, would you?"

"Frayed knot!"

• • •

284. A priest showed up at the local course on a Sunday morning. The caddie assigned to him said, "Hey, Father, what are you doing out here on a Sunday? Shouldn't you be giving a sermon or something?"

"It was such a beautiful day today, it was a toss-up whether I'd play golf or preach a sermon," said the priest. "I darn near wore my thumb out flipping, too!"

• • •

285. Angus and Haggis were sitting in the clubhouse at St. Andrews, in front of the fireplace on a raw, blustery day. The freezing rain was beating against the windows as their beards thawed out. Outside, the wind from the North Sea roared with gale force.

"That was some round of golf, eh?" said Angus, sipping on a scotch. "Same time next week, then?"

"Aye," said Haggis, "weather permitting."

• • •

286. An avid golfer had finally saved up enough money to fly to Scotland to play the sacred St. Andrews course. He had purchased a new outfit and new clubs before leaving and couldn't wait to tee off. Upon arriving for his tee time, he was paired with a local golfer. He confidently approached his ball, gripped his club, took a practice swing, and looked down the fairway. He then concentrated, pulled his club back, and took his first swing, missing the ball by a good two inches. He looked over to see the Scotsman shaking his head.

"That's weird," he said. "Your course must be about two inches lower than our course at home!"

• • •

PUTTING

287. A terrible golfer decides to take off work and spend the day at a plush country club playing golf. He hires a caddie and sets out for his game. He flubs shots and rips up sod all over the fairways, and he takes three times the normal amount of shots called for while putting.

By the eighteenth hole the golfer is furious and cussing quite loudly at his putting. He spots a lake off to the left of the fairway. He looks at the caddie and says, "I've putted so damn badly today, I think I'll go drown myself in that lake."

The caddie looks back at him and says, "I don't think you could keep your head down that long."

• • •

288. A female schoolteacher wanted to participate in her school's charity golf outing and decided to take some lessons. She had learned how to tee off and was now learning how to putt.

"Is the word spelled p-u-t or p-u-t-t?" she asked the instructor.

"P-u-t-t is the correct spelling," he replied. "P-u-t means to place something where you want it. At your rate, p-u-t-t is merely a vain attempt to do the same thing."

• • •

289. Three beginning golfers wanted to improve their putting game, so they each chipped in and decided to hire the golf pro from the local country club to give them private lessons. The pro showed them a few techniques and then demonstrated, sinking every putt. He then asked the three men to place their balls near the edge of the green and try a putt. One man tapped his ball way to the right, the other hit his off to the left, and the third guy pushed the ball all the way over to the other side of the green and into the rough.

After every attempt, the pro yelled at the guys, "LOFT!"

The guys finally looked at the pro and asked, "What the heck does 'loft' mean?"

The pro shouted, "Lack Of F$#%*@^ Talent!"

• • •

290. Simon wasn't having a good day on the golf course. After he missed three consecutive easy putts, his partner asked him what the problem was.

"Oh, it's my wife," said Simon. "She decided to take up golf, and since she's been playing, she's cut my sex down to once a week."

"You're lucky," said his partner. "She's cut some of us out altogether!"

• • •

291. A doctor and a psychiatrist meet at their country club for their usual Wednesday round of golf. The doctor has a little dog with him and on the first green, when he sinks a twenty-five-foot putt, the little dog starts yapping like crazy and jumping up and down on its hind legs.

The psychiatrist is quite amused by this and says, "Wow! That's one talented dog! What does he do if you miss a putt?"

"Flying somersaults," replies the doctor.

"Flying somersaults?" says the psychiatrist. "That's incredible! How many can he do?"

"It all depends on how hard I kick him in the ass!"

• • •

292. Two friends played golf together frequently and one was much better than the other. In spite of this, the lesser player was a good sport about it and never took strokes to even up the game; however, he always secretly vowed to find a way to get even.

One Saturday morning he showed up with a large gorilla at the first tee. He said to his friend, "I've been trying to beat you for a long time and almost gave up. That is, until I heard about this golfing gorilla. I'm sure you won't mind if he plays for me today. In fact, if you're game, I'd like to try to get back all the money I've lost to you this year. I figure that comes to about a thousand bucks. What do you say?"

The other guy laughed and said, "Let me get this straight. You want me to golf against a gorilla for a thousand dollars? Fine. After all, how good could a gorilla be at golf?"

The first hole was a slightly curved par-5 of 450 yards. The guy hit a beautiful tee shot 275 yards down the middle, leaving himself a 6-iron to the green. The gorilla took a few powerful practice swings and then laced the ball 450 yards with just enough hook to place it right at the pin, stopping it about four inches away from the hole.

The guy turns to his friend and says, "That's incredible! I never would've believed it if I hadn't seen it with my own eyes. Well, that settles it. I have no interest in being totally humiliated by a gorilla. You send this freakin' gorilla back to where he came from, and I'll meet you at the clubhouse for a drink and to write you a check."

After having a few drinks and handing over the check the guy asks, "By the way, how's that gorilla's putting?"

"Same as his driving."

"That good, huh?" the guy says.

"No, I mean he hits putts the same way—four hundred and fifty yards at a time!"

• • •

293. Two golf buddies sign up for a big golf tournament in Florida. They fly down to Florida and decide to have some drinks before the match to loosen up. They end up getting bombed out of their minds, and continue to drink during the match. Somehow they manage to stay even with their opponents through seventeen holes. In fact, on the eighteenth hole they're in a position to win the match if one of them can sink his six-foot putt.

The man sets up to putt with his feet wide apart. The crowd falls silent as he draws his putter back. Just then a squirrel comes running across the green being chased by a big black dog. The squirrel and dog go right between the guy's legs, out the other side, and off the green. The guy never flinches and strokes the ball into the hole to win the match! His partner goes wild and shouts, "I've never seen such total concentration. How did you manage to make that putt with that dog running between your legs?"

"Was that a real dog?"

• • •

294. An average golfer entered a three-day tournament and was assigned a caddie. On the first day, the golfer blew three key putts and ended with a bad opening score. The caddie said nothing. He tried to regroup on the second day but played even worse than the first, missing four putts. The caddie said nothing. Despite his best efforts, he messed up

almost every putt on the third day and wound up with a lousy final score for the tournament. The caddie was still silent. The golfer was livid and began swearing violently at the caddie. "You've got to be the worst caddie on earth!"

"Nah," deadpanned the caddie. "That'd be too much of a coincidence."

• • •

295. An old married couple are playing in their club's annual senior couples tournament. As luck would have it, they end up playing in a playoff hole and it is down to a six-inch putt that the wife has to make for the match. The wife eyes up the putt, calmly takes her stance, and concentrates. She swings, misses the putt, and they lose the match. On the way home her husband is fuming, "I can't believe you missed that damn putt! That putt was no longer than my willy."

The wife returns the husband's look and smirks. "Yeah, but it was much harder!"

• • •

296. A priest and one of his parishioners decided to play golf after church one Sunday. On the third hole the parishioner blew a simple six-foot putt and said, "Oh, damn it all!"

The priest looked at him and said, "Now, now. Instead of cussing, why not say, 'Lord, give me strength'?"

The guy apologized and set up for his next attempt at the putt. After blowing a simple seven-footer, the guy again burst out, "Damn it—why me?"

"Ah, ah," said the priest. "Remember what I said. Say, 'Lord, give me strength.'"

The guy set up for his final attempt at the putt, and just before taking his swing said, "Lord, give me strength." All of a sudden the ball started spinning, rolled straight for the hole, and fell in. The guy said, "Hey, Father. What do you know about that?"

The priest stared in amazement and replied, "Well, I'll be damned!"

• • •

297. Every Sunday during prayers at the church service, an avid golfer would say a little prayer for his golfing companion of ten years. "Please, dear Lord," he would begin, "watch over my friend and best buddy, and keep him safe for another week." After two years of this his wife finally asked why he prayed for his friend each week.

"Are you kidding?" exclaimed the golfer. "If anything happened to him I'd be the worst putter at the club!"

• • •

298. Two golfers and their caddies were out on the course one day. By the fifteenth hole the first golfer had blown so many putts he went berserk. He started swearing out loud, grabbed his putter, and, with a mighty toss, threw it at the water hazard forty yards away.

One caddie turned to the other and said, "Five bucks says he misses the water."

• • •

299. A decent golfer was having a bad day when it came to putting. Every putt seemed to stop one or two rolls from the cup. "What the heck am I doing wrong?" cried the golfer out loud.

"It's simple," said his partner. "You're playing American rules with a Russian ball."

"What's a Russian ball?" asked the golfer.

"A Russian ball is one that always needs another revolution."

• • •

300. A seasoned tour pro was having the worst day of his career when it came to putting one day. Every time he lined up what he thought was the perfect putt, the ball would break too far left or right, lip the cup and roll out, or skip completely over the cup. Finally fed up after having missed a simple two-footer on the fourteenth green, he let out a loud expletive. Immediately the tournament marshals confronted him and handed him a one-hundred-dollar fine.

"You're going to fine me for one lousy curse word?" said the pro.

"Those are the tour rules," said one of the marshals.

"Fine," he said, reaching into his wallet. "Here's an extra five hundred to cover this, you no-good F&*^%$#, *&^ -), *@&#!!!!"

• • •

301. Two friends met up in the clubhouse after a round of golf, and were discussing their games. "This is a pretty tough course," said the first. "How'd you do today?"

"Oh, the usual," said the second. "I'm a pre-putt-par."

"What the heck is that?" asked the second.

"It means I shoot par on the fairway and four-putt on the green!"

• • •

302. Two guys were on the green of the twelfth hole getting set to putt. Out of nowhere a golf ball came bounding at them and stopped four inches from the cup. One of the guys said, "Watch me have a little fun with this guy." And with that, he tapped the ball into the hole with his putter. A few seconds later a guy appeared.

"Hey, look, mister," said the golfer, "you got the ball into the cup!"

The other golfer started jumping up and down and said, "Hey, you guys, hurry up over here and see this. I got a ten!"

• • •

303. Four friends were sitting around the clubhouse describing what each thought was the most difficult shot in all of golf.

"It has to be the pitching from the rough on eighteen at Augusta for the Masters," said the first.

"Nope," said the second. "The toughest is teeing up at the last hole at the U.S. Open."

"No way," said the third. "The worst is a two-iron shot to win the British Open."

"Wrong, wrong, wrong," said the fourth. "The hardest shot in all of golf is a four-foot putt being watched by the guy sitting on the lawnmower, waiting to finish grooming the course!"

• • •

304. A golfer came home from the course ranting and raving about the lousy day he had.

"Now what's wrong?" said his wife.

"That SOB partner of mine wouldn't concede a three-foot putt," said the golfer.

"So, how hard could a three-footer be?" she asked.

"Are you kidding? It cost me two strokes!"

• • •

305. A golfer who had blown yet another putt looked up to the heavens and screamed, "What are You doing to me! I dare You to come down here and fight fair! And for that matter, bring Your Old Man, I don't care. Heck, we can even play best ball!"

• • •

306. A guy walked into the clubhouse with a dejected look on his face, one of many such golfers. A friend came up to him and asked, "Say, Gregg, why the long face?"

The golfer, still looking down, said, "I putted so poorly today that one of the guys I was paired with asked me if my husband played golf!"

• • •

RELIGION

307. A golfer is playing a serious round with a close friend who is ahead by a couple of strokes. The golfer says to himself, "Man, I'd give anything to sink this next putt."

A tall stranger walks up to him and whispers, "Would you give up a fourth of your sex life?" The golfer believes the man is crazy and that his answer will be meaningless, but thinks what the heck, so he says, "Okay," and sinks the putt.

Two holes later he mumbles to himself, "Boy, if I could only get an eagle on this hole." The same stranger appears and says, "Would it be worth another fourth of your sex life?" The golfer shrugs and says, "Sure, why not?" He makes an eagle.

On the final hole, the golfer needs another eagle to win. He says nothing, but the stranger reappears and says, "Would you be willing to give up the rest of your sex life to win this match?" The golfer says, "Certainly!" He makes the eagle.

As the golfer walks back to the clubhouse the stranger appears and says, "You know, I've really not been fair with you. I'm actually the devil, and from now on you'll have no sex life."

"Nice to meet you," says the golfer. "By the way, I'm Father O'Malley."

• • •

308. There was a priest from a large parish who was an avid golfer. Every chance he could get, he would head for the golf course and play as many holes as possible. Golf was his true passion. One sunny, warm Sunday morning the priest was overcome with the desire to play golf. He called the deacon to tell him that he was sick and could not conduct church services. Then he packed up the car and drove three hours to a golf course where no one would recognize him.

An angel from above was watching the preacher and was quite perturbed. He went to God and said, "Look at that priest. He should be punished for what he is doing."

God nodded in agreement and set a plan in motion. The priest teed up on the first hole and hit a beautiful shot that sailed effortlessly through the air and landed right in the cup 350 yards away. The priest was shocked and elated. The rest of his game continued in the same way, and at the end, the priest realized he had broken every course record.

The angel was a little confused and said, "Begging Your pardon, but I thought You were going to punish him."

God smiled. "Think about it. Who's he going to tell?"

• • •

309. Moses, Jesus, and another guy were out playing golf one day. Moses set up his tee shot and drove a long one. It landed in the fairway but rolled directly toward a water hazard. Moses quickly raised his club, the water parted, and the ball rolled to the other side safe and sound.

Next, Jesus hit a nice long shot and it started to head toward the same water hazard. All of a sudden it stopped dead in the middle of the water and just hovered there on top. Jesus casually walked out onto the pond and chipped it up onto the green.

The third guy set up his shot and took a wild whack at the ball. It headed out over a fence, directly into oncoming traffic on a nearby street. It bounced off a truck and landed on a nearby house where it rolled into the gutter, down the spout, out onto the fairway, and right toward the same water hazard.

On the way to the trap, it hit a little stone and bounced out over the water onto a lily pad where a very large bullfrog swallowed it. Just then an eagle swooped down, grabbed the frog, and flew away. As it passed over the green the frog threw up and dropped the ball, which bounced right into the hole for a beautiful hole in one.

Moses then turned to Jesus and said, "I hate playing with your dad."

• • •

310. The pope met with the College of Cardinals to discuss a proposal from Shimon Peres, the former leader of Israel. "Your holiness," said one of the cardinals, "Mr. Peres wants to determine whether Jews or Catholics are superior by challenging you to a golf match." The pope was worried, as he had never before played golf.

"Not to worry," said the cardinal, "We'll call America and talk to Jack Nicklaus. We'll make him a cardinal and he can play Shimon Peres. We can't lose!" Everyone agreed it was a good idea. The call was made and, of course, Jack was honored and agreed to play.

The day after the match, Nicklaus reported to the Vatican to inform the pope of his success in the match. "I came in second, Your Holiness," said Nicklaus.

"Second?" exclaimed the surprised pope. "You came in second to Shimon Peres?"

"No," said Nicklaus, "second to Rabbi Woods."

• • •

311. An avid golfer died and awoke to find himself at the Pearly Gates, looking up at St. Peter. "Ah," says St. Peter, "we've been expecting you. Let me look through my entrance book. Hmmm. You've had a good life, but I see you sometimes used profanity while golfing."

"Well, um, yes," said the man sheepishly.

"Well, I've been known to make an exception when there are special circumstances."

"Well," said the man, "as you know, I was a golfer."

"Go ahead, son, tell me what happened," said St. Peter.

"Well, I was playing in a big tournament and had a one-stroke lead. As I started my backswing for my drive on the last hole, I realized I had the five-iron instead of the four-iron."

"So that's when you swore?" asked St. Peter.

"Well, no, as it turned out I hit the five-iron shot of my life! The ball was headed straight for the fairway, when all of a sudden a passing bird flew into the ball's path."

"Ah, so that's when you cursed?" asked St. Peter.

"Well, not exactly. Just as the bird got to the ball it started to hook and the bird actually helped direct the ball toward the green. It landed and started to roll toward the cup when all of a sudden a groundhog came onto the green and ran toward my ball."

An angry St. Peter said, "Surely, that's when you cursed!"

"Not exactly," said the man. "The groundhog actually pushed the ball toward the hole, where it stopped rolling just about five inches from the cup."

St. Peter screamed, "YOU DIDN'T MISS THE F^$%ING PUTT, DID YOU?"

• • •

312. A man and his priest are playing in a golf match. The man's game is perfect that day, but the priest is having a terrible time on every hole. Sensing the priest's unhappiness, the man says, "Cheer up, Father. Just think, one of these days you will be giving the services at my funeral."

The priest looks at him without a grin and replies, "You may be right, but it will still be your hole."

• • •

313. Three conservative rabbis with long beards were playing golf one Wednesday afternoon. A priest named Father Mahoney also came to play golf that day and was assigned to the threesome by the head ranger. So, he joined the rabbis and played eighteen holes. At the end of the game his score was 114, while the rabbis shot 68, 71, and 72. He said to the rabbis, "How come you all play such good

golf?" The first rabbi said, "When you live a religious life and attend temple such as we do, you are rewarded."

Father Mahoney loved golf so much that he decided to convert and join a temple. He attended services twice a week and led an exceptionally holy life. About a year later he met the three rabbis for another game of golf. This time he shot 102, while the rabbis shot a 67, 69, and 71.

He said to them, "I don't get it. I joined a temple, I live a religious life, and I'm still playing lousy golf."

The first rabbi said to him, "What temple did you join?"

"Beth Shalom."

"Schmuck! That one's for tennis!"

• • •

314. A lifelong golfer dies and finds himself at the gates of heaven. St. Peter greets him and tells him that there's all the golf he could want in heaven. In fact, he has a tee time at heaven's replica course of Pebble Beach and that some of his old golfing friends are already at the tee waiting for him. To make it even better, he is told that he has a starting time the next morning at the replica of St. Andrews and that he can check in after that for his future starting times.

He joins his old friends and has a fine day at Pebble. He shoots so-so, but is striking the ball well, has back his old vigor, and is ready to go the next morning at St. Andrews. When he checks in the next day, St. Peter inquires about his game and asks him, "Well, how do you like it so far?"

"I like it a lot, St. Peter," says the golfer. "This is fantastic. If it hadn't been for all that health food my wife fed me, I could have been here ten years ago!"

• • •

315. A rabbi and a priest go golfing with two other friends one afternoon. Before the one friend gets up to hit the ball, he crosses himself. The rabbi leans over to the priest to ask, "What does that mean?"

The priest responds, "Not a damned thing if he can't play!"

• • •

316. Jesus and Moses are out playing one sunny day when they come to a long par-4 over water. Moses pulls out a 5-iron and hits a nice shot to the green, leaving himself a seventeen-foot putt. Jesus tees his ball up and says, "You know, Jack Nicklaus would probably hit a perfect seven-iron, so that's what I'll use." He hits the ball right into the middle of the pond. He thinks for a moment and then looks over at Moses, who says, "All right, Lord, here you go." With that the water parts and Jesus retrieves his ball. Again, Jesus tees it up, saying, "I'm positive Jack would use a seven-iron for this shot." Again, he hits it into the middle of the pond. Moses, getting somewhat frustrated, parts the water for him again. As Jesus tees it up for the third time, Moses says, "All right, Lord, this time You're on Your own." Sure enough, Jesus drops the ball right into the middle of the pond.

While Jesus is walking on the water to the middle of the pond looking for his ball, another twosome arrives at the tee. One of them walks up next to Moses and says, "Who does that guy think he is, Jesus Christ?"

Moses replies, "No, He knows He's Jesus Christ. He *thinks* He's Jack Nicklaus!"

• • •

317. Three avid golfers happened to meet at the Pearly Gates one morning while waiting for St. Peter. St. Peter finally arrived and told them that through the gates of heaven was the greatest golf course ever created. He also said that each man would be given a set of golf clubs based on how faithful each had been in his marriage. The first man admitted to St. Peter that he had cheated on his wife twice. St. Peter said that it was a bad thing that he did, so he gave him a middle-of-the-line set of clubs. The second man told St. Peter that he had cheated on his wife once. St. Peter said that it was a bad thing that he did, but since he only did it once, he gave him a pretty decent set of clubs. The third man said to St. Peter that he had never cheated on his wife

and was happily married for fifty years. St. Peter gave this man a set of Big Bertha oversize clubs and irons.

A few days later the first two men were setting up to tee off on the first hole when they noticed the third man with his Big Bertha clubs, sitting on the side of the fairway crying. "What in the world are you crying about? You got the best set of clubs," said one of the men.

"I know I should be happy, but I just saw my wife coming off the eighteenth and all she had was a five-iron and a putter."

• • •

318. An angry golfer came into the clubhouse for a quick bite and started telling the bartender about his game. "I was having the game of a lifetime. All I needed was to sink a six-inch putt to clinch the match. It was no more than a tap-in. The green was perfectly flat, there was no breeze, and it was quiet. I gently hit the ball and it was rolling straight for the cup. Then all of a sudden a bird swooped down, snatched my ball, flew over a pond, and dropped my ball right in the middle." St. Peter ended with a sigh, "That's the last time I play golf with St. Francis of Assisi."

• • •

319. Satan called a meeting of his fiendish cabinet to complain about Hades becoming too soft an option due to complacency and idleness. "You guys and all your junior devil charges have to tighten up, crack down, and give our eternal guests one *Hell* of a time. Do you understand?" snapped Satan. "I want them tested to the limit! I want them tormented, humiliated, discouraged, and beaten, all the while giving them false hope that things will get better!"

"Oh, you mean like it is in golf," replied one staff member.

"Now, wait a minute," said Satan with caution. "Nothing *that* strong. I mean, they're only human and they have to last us forever!"

• • •

320. A hacker found himself paired with a priest one Saturday at the local club. The hacker couldn't help but notice that before every shot, the priest would cross himself and whisper a short prayer. It must have helped because the priest was shooting a great game. Finally, on the twelfth hole the hacker said, "Father, do you think if I said a prayer before each shot I would be a better golfer?"

"No, my son," said the priest. "I don't think it will help."

"Why is that, Father?" asked the hack.

"Because, my son, you're a lousy golfer!"

• • •

321. It was a mild, sunny morning when the foursome met for their weekly round. The group was finishing up their first hole when one noticed some dark clouds gathering far away on the horizon. "Gee, I hope they don't come this way," he said.

"Don't worry about it, just keep playing," said another.

By the third hole, the clouds were getting darker and closer, and a rumble of thunder could be heard. "Hey, guys, don't you think we should think about stopping at nine?" suggested the golfer.

"Don't worry. Now let's just keep playing!" snapped another.

By the ninth hole, the storm clouds were nearly overhead, the temperature had dropped ten degrees, and the wind had picked up considerably. Just then there was a huge clap of thunder and a bolt of lightning that struck a tree fifty feet behind them.

"That's it! I'm outa here!" said the golfer, grabbing his golf bag and leaving. "When God wants to play through, you don't argue with Him!"

• • •

322. A foursome of regulars teed off promptly at 7:30 one beautiful Sunday morning. As they headed down the fairway it grew eerily dark all of a sudden. They looked up and saw a freak black cloud directly above. A bolt of lightning shot toward them and the next thing they knew they were standing at the gates of heaven. St. Peter looked at his book and said, "Ah, the Wilson foursome. You're right on time. You may enter."

"Um, excuse me, Your Excellence, but we're the Buchanan foursome," said one of the golfers sheepishly.

"What?" came a mighty roar. "That's impossible. You teed off at 7:30. You must be the Wilson foursome."

"No, sir. One of the Wilson foursome arrived late so we took their tee time. They teed off at 7:40."

"Oh, dear, dear," said St. Peter. "This isn't good. I'm going to have to send you back."

"Send us back?" exclaimed one of the men. "We're dead. How are we going to explain that to our wives and families?"

"I'm sorry, I have no choice in the matter," said St. Peter. "However, for all that you've been through, I'll grant one wish for the four of you."

The foursome huddled and whispered among themselves for about five minutes before turning back to St. Peter.

"Well, then, gentlemen. Have you decided upon your wish?"

"Yes, sir," said one of the men. "We'd like to go back as transvestites."

"What? Why in the world would you like to go back as transvestites?"

"Well, this way we can shoot from the red tees and still have sex with women!"

• • •

323. After a long wait, it was time for the annual "Heavenly Golf Championship." Team captains for that year's competition, as chosen by the Almighty Himself, were St. Peter and Jesus. A crowd had formed on the heavenly green early in the morning in anticipation of the event. Every newscaster in heaven was broadcasting the event, and every sportswriter was there with his pencil and paper in hand. The two teams met near the first tee for warm-ups and practice swings. St. Peter looked over Jesus' team and said, "Hmm. They look pretty good this year. I better call up reinforcements." With that, a huge bolt of lightning shot down to earth from heaven, followed by a loud rumble of thunder. Then a representative from St. Peter's team walked over to Jesus and handed him a new roster.

"Hey," said Jesus. "Who's this new guy? He wasn't on the original team roster."

St. Peter hollered over, grinning, "Oh, that's Archbishop Palmer. New arrival."

"Oh, really," said Jesus, gesturing toward the Earth with one arm. A tremendous bolt of lightning shot down, followed by another roar of thunder. "Then, I'd like you to meet my new team member, Cardinal Nicklaus!"

• • •

324. A man was paired up with a priest one Saturday morning at the local course. It didn't take long for the golfer to real-

ize that the priest was a hack golfer. At the first hole, the priest drove his tee shot into the woods, then let out with a string of bad words. "Father!" exclaimed the golfer.

"Sorry, my son," said the priest.

On the third hole the priest dropped three balls in the water hazard, and let loose with another string of profanities. "Father! Watch your language!" said the golfer.

"Please forgive me, my son." murmured the priest.

By the fourteenth hole the priest had had enough. He threw his clubs in the drink and started to walk off the course. "This just isn't going to work. I have no alternative but to give it up," he declared.

The man looked astonished. "Father, you're going to give up golf?"

"No, the priesthood!" he said. "It's obvious I don't have a prayer!"

• • •

325. A priest was paired with a young man at the local club one Saturday. The priest said, "I love the game of golf, but I'm not very good at it. You'll have to be patient with me."

"No problem," said the young man. "I'm a golf pro from out of town. Maybe I can teach you a few things."

Throughout the whole game the pro would offer suggestions to the priest about how to hold his club, how to stand, how to keep his left arm straight, etc. The priest thanked the young man at the end of the round as they were walking off the course.

"Ah, wait a minute, Father," he said. "You owe me fifty dollars."

"What?" said the priest, astonished. "Fifty dollars for what?"

"Well, I am a golf pro and this is how I make my living," said the pro. "After all, I did teach you quite a few things today."

The priest begrudgingly agreed and said, "I don't have that much cash on me now. Why don't you stop by the church tomorrow morning and I'll pay you then. And while you're at it, bring your mother and father."

"Why do you need them?" asked the upstart pro.

"Don't you think it's about time they were married?"

• • •

326. A guy has been golfing at the local club for twenty years and has never broken par on the fifteenth hole. Finally, in a fit of frustration, the golfer screams up at the heavens, "God, why, oh, why can't I break par on this one hole just once before I die?"

With that the ground beneath him shakes, and a mighty voice calls to him saying, "Next week you will receive your answer."

So, next week at the fifteenth, he tees up his ball and waits . . . nothing. He hits a decent enough shot, goes to where his ball is, and waits. Just as he is about to hit his second shot a voice calls down from heaven, "Use the five-wood."

The guy looks up and says, "But this is a three-wood shot." The ground vibrates once more. He immediately goes back to his bag and gets the 5-wood. He reaches into his bag and opens a new sleeve of balls. The ground shakes again and the voice says, "Don't make me laugh."

• • •

327. A priest was enjoying a decent round of golf one Saturday morning. He had just broken par on the fourth hole and was driving his cart to a narrow bridge that led to the fifth. All of a sudden, from out of nowhere came another cart at top speed from behind some trees. The resulting crash pushed both carts onto the narrow bridge. The carts toppled over the side and the bridge came down with them. The men stood up, both shook their heads, and tried to regain their composure. Sloshing over to the other driver, the priest asked, "Are you all right? I didn't see you come out from behind the trees. I guess I was too excited about beating the last hole. By the way, my name's Father Williams."

"Thanks," said the other driver. "I'm fine. I, too, am a man of the cloth. My name is Rabbi Lipschitz."

They looked around for a moment and started picking

up their respective equipment. "Eureka!" shouted the rabbi. "My bottle of wine for tonight's temple service wasn't broken in the crash. I keep it with me so it doesn't get too warm in my car. This must be a sign from God Almighty. Let's drink a toast to celebrate that neither of us was injured in the crash."

The rabbi handed the priest the bottle. The priest took a long drink, wiped the rim, and handed the bottle back to the rabbi. The rabbi then put the cap back on the bottle.

"Aren't you going to have any?" inquired the priest.

"No, I think I'll wait for the police!"

• • •

328. A rabbi and a priest were paired up one Saturday morning for a game at the local club. The priest was having a terrible round, and every time he flubbed a shot, he let loose with a string of obscenities.

"Father," said the rabbi, "Your language is certainly not becoming of a man of your education and religious teachings. If you're not careful, God will strike you down."

The priest just mumbled incoherently at the rabbi's words and continued playing. On the seventeenth hole the priest sliced his tee shot way off into the woods. Completely frustrated, the priest threw his clubs, kicked his bag, and began another cussing tirade. With that, the ground shook, the sky darkened, and a huge bolt of lightning shot down and killed the rabbi dead.

Just then a powerful voice was heard from above, "*$^#^@, I missed!"

• • •

329. Two golfers are taking a breather at the refreshment stand between the ninth and tenth holes.

"So, I'm taking my wife to the Holy Land to walk where the saints once did," said the first.

"Wow, you're taking her to Jerusalem?" said the second.

"Jerusalem! Whatever gave you an idea like that? I'm taking her to St. Andrews!"

• • •

330. At the end of the Sunday morning high mass at the local Catholic church, the priest had his head down praying for what seemed like an eternity. In fact, some of the parishioners thought there might be something wrong with him. A wife leaned over to her husband and whispered, "Boy, he sure is praying hard today. He must have a lot on his mind."

"Praying, nothing," said the husband. "We're playing golf later and he's just practicing keeping his head down."

• • •

331. One day a loudmouthed, arrogant, hack golfer died while on the back nine of his club's course. He suddenly found himself in a hallway with two doors, one made of gold, the other made of coal. A little old man was sitting behind a small desk in between the two doors.

"Hey, old man, what gives? What is this place?" asked the hack.

"Ah, Mr. Novell, we've been expecting you," said the old man. "You died playing golf today and now you have to choose one door or the other. The gold door is heaven, the other . . . well, you get the picture."

"Do they got golf in both places?" demanded the hack.

"Oh my, yes," said the old man in a macabre voice. "Let me show you the course that awaits you through each door."

So the old man took him through heaven's door to look at the course and, much to the hack's surprise, it wasn't all that much to look at. The fairways were narrow, the grass was a bit too high, and the greens looked as if they could use some water. They went through hell's door, and the guy was awed by the course. There were beautiful greens, gently rolling hills, not too many bunkers, and a refreshment stand every two holes.

"I'll take this one!" exclaimed the hack.

"Excellent choice, sir. Damian here will be your guide."

The hack followed Damian into the clubhouse, where he was suited up with brand-new clothes, new shoes, and a new tam. They got out to the first tee and the guy couldn't

112

believe he was there. The two of them just stood there for a minute or two. Growing impatient, the man said, "Now what?"

"Now what, what?" asked Damian in a sinister voice.

"Where are my clubs? Where are my balls?" demanded the hack.

Damian bellowed a haunting laugh and shouted, "There aren't any!"

• • •

332. A hack golfer was putting on the thirteenth hole at Pebble Beach when he died of a heart attack. He awoke to find himself being greeted by St. Peter at the Pearly Gates. "Welcome to heaven," said St. Peter. "St. Michael here will be your tour guide."

St. Michael led the hack golfer to many beautiful places, including some of the best golf courses he had ever seen. Next to the grillroom there was a large room with what seemed to be a million clocks on the wall. "What are all these?" asked the golfer.

"Ah, these," said St. Michael. "These are dial indicators for all the golfers who have joined us this year. The more a golfer cussed on Earth, the faster the hands move."

"Wow, that's incredible," said the golfer. "Where's mine?"

"Yours?" said St. Michael, "I'm afraid they use yours for a fan in the kitchen!"

• • •

333. Three hack golfing buddies who were known for womanizing, being mean, and dirty dealings were out on the course one day when a tremendous bolt of lightning struck and killed them. They awoke to find themselves in hell, standing near an ugly, gnarled-up demon. "You three have led terrible lives and now you will pay the consequences in hell," said the demon. "Each of you follow me."

The demon led them down a corridor to three doors. "There is one door for each of you," said the demon. "Who will be first to enter his fate for eternity?"

Two of the golfers pushed the third a bit forward. The

demon opened the door to reveal a crumpled, beat-up golf bag full of broken club pieces and split golf balls all resting in a heap near an overgrown golf course. At once the hack was whisked into the domain with the door slamming closed behind him. The other two stared in horror. Another golfer stepped forward to meet his fate. Through his door was pretty much the same thing. The third golfer walked over and opened his door. There stood a beautiful female golf pro, with two sets of Ping clubs, next to a beautifully groomed golf course.

The golfer jumped up and down with excitement.

The demon looked at the woman and said, "Miss, you have sinned. . . ."

• • •

SEX

---

334. A guy decides to spend every day of his vacation golfing. First thing Monday morning he sets off on his first round and soon catches up to the person ahead, who turns out to be a very attractive lady. He takes an interest in her and suggests that they play the rest of the round together. She agrees and the round continues. It turns out that she's not only very attractive, but a very talented golfer and she wins their little competition on the last hole.

He congratulates her and then offers to give her a lift home. All in all, it's been a very enjoyable morning. On the way to her place she thanks him for sharing his morning with her and for the competition and says she hasn't enjoyed herself so much on the course for a long time. "In fact," she says, "I'd like you to pull over so I can show you how much I appreciated everything." He pulls over, she kisses him full on the lips for thirty seconds, and then things progress from there.

The next morning he sees his new friend at the first tee and suggests they play together again. He's actually quite competitive and anxious to prove he can beat her at golf. They have another magnificent day enjoying each other's company and playing a tight, competitive round of golf. She beats him on the last hole, and again he drives her home and again she shows her appreciation in the car.

This goes on all week, with her beating him by a narrow margin every day. By this time, though, he doesn't mind so much. In fact, during the car ride home from their Friday morning round, he tells her that he has had such an enjoyable week that he's planned a romantic dinner for two at a fancy candlelit restaurant followed by a night of passion in the penthouse apartment of a posh hotel.

Surprisingly, she bursts into tears and says she can't go through with it. He can't understand what all the fuss is about and finally gets her to explain.

"I really like you," she cries, "but I'm a transvestite."

"A transvestite!?" he shrieks. He swerves the car violently off the road, pulls it to a screeching halt, and curses madly, overcome with emotion.

"I'm sorry," she repeats.

"You bastard!" he screams, turning beet red in the face. "You dirty, cheating bastard! You've been playing off the red tees all week!"

• • •

335. A grandfather, father, and son are ready to tee off on the first tee for a nice round of golf for their traditional Father's Day outing. Just as they are about to take the first swing, a beautiful, well-endowed blonde walks up to the tee and explains that the ranger told her to join them. Expecting the worst, but being polite, the three reluctantly agree.

As they wait for her to hit her first tee shot, the three men joke that she might be able "play," but not golf. To their surprise she belts a 215-yard drive, passing all three of them. "Well, this might not be too bad after all," Gramps says. Throughout the entire round she is hitting unbelievably well, driving, chipping, and putting. On the eighteenth green she is left with a six-foot putt for birdie, which would give her the best round ever. She thinks for a moment and says, "I'll give a blow job to whichever of you three can give me the best advice on how to sink this putt right after this round!"

Well, you'd think they had just won the lottery, they all get so excited. The grandson studies the putt and tells her it breaks five inches to the left. The dad walks over, then behind, eyes it from every angle, then walks back behind the ball and says, "No, you're wrong. It will break seven inches to the right."

Gramps just smiles, hobbles over to the ball, makes sure no one is looking, picks up the ball, and says, "It's a gimme!"

• • •

336. A guy gets stranded on a desert island and is all alone for ten years. One day, he sees a speck on the horizon. He thinks to himself, "It's not a ship." The speck gets a little closer and he mutters, "It doesn't look like a boat." The speck gets even closer and he thinks, "It doesn't even look like a raft." Then, out of the surf comes a gorgeous blonde woman wearing a wetsuit and scuba gear. She approaches the guy and says, "How long has it been since you've had a good smoke?"

"Ten years," he says.

She reaches over and unzips a waterproof pocket on her left sleeve and pulls out a fresh Cuban cigar and a lighter. He lights it, takes a long drag, and says, "Man, oh, man! Is that good!"

Then she asks, "How long has it been since you've had a drink of fine cognac?"

"Ten years," he replies.

She reaches over, unzips the waterproof pocket on her right sleeve, pulls out a small flask, and gives it to him. He takes a long swig and says, "Wow, Remy Martin XO. That's fantastic!" Then she starts unzipping the long zipper that runs down the front of her wet suit and says to him, "And how long has it been since you've had some *real* fun?"

The man replies, "My God! Don't tell me that you've got golf clubs in there!"

• • •

337. A man was playing a game of golf, and on the fourteenth hole he hit the ball right into a big field of buttercups. Being an honest golfer, he picked up the ball and laid it next to the flower bed to avoid destroying the beautiful buttercups. Just then a fairy appeared and said, "Thank you for not disturbing my buttercups. For that I shall make sure that you always have a full supply of butter."

"Thank you," the golfer replied, "but where were you last week when I hit the ball into the pussy willows?"

• • •

338. A man plays hookie from work and decides to go out golfing. He is on the third hole when he notices a bullfrog sitting next to the green. He thinks nothing of it and is about to shoot when he hears, "Ribbit. Nine-iron."

The man looks around and doesn't see anyone, so he sets up for his shot again. "Ribbit. Nine-iron." He looks at the frog and thinks, "It can't be!" He decides to find out. He puts down his 7-iron, grabs a 9-iron, and hits a birdie. He's shocked. He says to the bullfrog, "Wow! That's pretty amazing! You must be a lucky bullfrog, eh?"

The bullfrog replies, "Ribbit. Lucky frog. Lucky frog."

The man thinks for a moment, then decides to take the frog with him to the next hole. "Okay, frog, what do you think?"

"Ribbit. Three-wood." The guy takes out a 3-wood and gets a hole in one. The man is dumbfounded and doesn't know what to say.

By the end of the day the man has golfed the best game of his life. He looks at the frog and says, "Now what?"

"Ribbit. Las Vegas."

So the man packs up the frog and some clothes and heads for Las Vegas. "Okay, frog. Now what?"

"Ribbit. Roulette. Three thousand on black six."

It is a million-to-one shot that this black six will win, but after the golf game, the man figures, "What the heck." Black six comes in and tons of cash come sliding back across the table.

The man takes his winnings and gets the best room in the hotel. He sits down next to the frog and says, "How can I ever repay you? First I golf the best game of my life, and now this!"

"Ribbit. Kiss Me."

The guy figures, why not? After all the frog has done for him the amphibian deserves it. So, he kisses the frog. All of a sudden, the frog turns into the most gorgeous sixteen-year-old girl in the world.

"And that, Mr. Starr, is how the sixteen-year-old girl ended up in my room."

• • •

339. A golfer was teeing off on the fifth at Augusta when he noticed a small bottle protruding from the ground. He dug out the bottle, pulled out the cork, and a small genie appeared. "I will grant you one wish," said the genie. The man thought a while and said, "Well, I've always been embarrassed by being rather small, if you know what I mean. Could you make me more manly? You know, larger?"

"Consider it done." And with that the genie disappeared. Continuing with his game, the man noticed an immediate change in his size. In fact, by the twelfth hole it was down to his knees, and by the eighteenth he was sure it was peeking through the bottom of his pant leg. After finishing his final putt, the man raced back to where he'd met the genie. "Genie! Genie! Where are you!?"

"Problem?" inquired the genie. "Yes," said the man. "Do you think I could trouble you for just one more wish?"

"And what might that be?" asked the genie.

"Longer legs!"

• • •

340. A man was waiting to play on the fifth tee when the woman in front of him lost her grip on her club while in full backswing. The club hurdled wildly toward him and hit him. He groaned and doubled over in pain, clasping his hand to his crotch.

The woman quickly ran over to the man and started apologizing. "I am *so* sorry. This has never happened before. Here, let me help you." The woman opened the man's pants and began fondling and stroking him. After a minute she asked, "There. Is that any better?"

The man said, "Oh yes, that's great, but my thumb still hurts like crazy!"

• • •

341. A businessman traveled to Japan to play golf with a few Japanese business associates. Having no meetings the night before his big game, he decided to solicit the services of a prostitute.

Just when things started to get very passionate, she suddenly screamed out, "Mitzukawi!" Not knowing the translation, he figured it meant he was performing exceptionally well, and so he kept going.

A few seconds later she screamed, "Mitzukawi! Mitzukawi!" He smiled proudly and thought to himself, "Man, I must be really good!"

Finally, she shrieked, "Mitzukawi!" a third time, jumped out of bed, and ran from the room without getting paid. "Must have been too good for her!" he thought to himself and went to sleep.

The next day, while in the middle of his round of golf, one of his Japanese associates hit a perfect 7-iron off the tee right into the cup for a hole in one! Wanting to impress his associates with his new word, the man yelled out, "Mitzukawi!"

Perplexed, the Japanese golfer turned to him and asked, "What do you mean, wrong hole?"

• • •

342. A businessman and his secretary were having a torrid affair. One afternoon they decided to get a motel room and have passionate sex all afternoon. He wasn't used to the exercise and fell asleep afterward, not waking up until about 9:00 that night.

He jumped up in a panic when he realized it was so late. He told his receptionist, "Quick! While I get dressed, take my shoes outside and drag them around through the grass and mud. Don't ask questions, just do it."

The man got home at about 10:00 and his wife confronted him at the door asking where he had been. The man said, "I can't lie to you. I spent the better part of the day making passionate love to my receptionist in a motel room; then I fell asleep. When I woke up and saw what time it was I rushed right home."

The woman looked down at his muddy shoes and said, "You lying SOB! You've been out playing golf again!"

• • •

343. A woman decides to take up golf. After three months of trying to teach herself and still playing quite badly, she decides to consult a golf pro.

She explains to the pro how bad she is and he tells her to go ahead and hit the ball. She takes a whack at the ball and it only goes about fifty yards and into the brush. The pro says, "I can see that you have a lot of problems. First, your stance is bad, and second, your head is all over the place. But the worst thing is your grip."

When she asks the pro for advice, he says, "Grab the club gently, as if you were grabbing your husband's penis. When the feeling is right, go ahead and swing away." She does exactly what he suggests and she hits the ball perfectly straight for about 225 yards.

The golf pro looks at the woman and says, "That's incredible! I didn't think you would do that well. Of course, now we have to figure out how to get the club out of your mouth!"

• • •

344. Five statements that golf talk and phone sex have in common:
   1. Darn, I bent my shaft.
   2. Keep your head down and spread your legs a bit more.
   3. Mind if I join your threesome?
   4. My hands are so sweaty I can't get a good grip.
   5. Wait a minute, I need to wash my balls first.

• • •

345. A psychiatrist and a urologist decided to meet up for a round of golf one Wednesday. The urologist always seemed to hit his drives right down the middle of the fairway, while the psychiatrist always hooked his ball completely off the fairway. He asked the urologist for some suggestions. The urologist said, "Well, I don't see anything wrong with your swing; perhaps I should give you a physical to determine the problem." The next day the shrink came to the doctor's office for an exam. "Well," said the doctor, "I see your problem. Your penis is three times longer than the average male's. It's obviously causing an anomaly in your swing."

"Can you fix it?" asked the shrink.

"Yes, but it will mean surgery," said the doctor.

The shrink loved golf more than life and told the doctor to do whatever it took.

Six weeks later they met for another round of golf. The shrink teed up his ball on the first hole and hit a perfect shot that landed ten feet from the cup. The doctor teed up his first shot and addressed the ball. The shrink, overcome with curiosity, asked the doctor what happened to the extra "parts" that were removed. The doctor swung, smiled, and watched his shot hook two fairways away.

• • •

346. A foursome of regulars was standing waiting to hit on the first tee when one of the men said he wouldn't be able to play for the next five weeks. "What do you mean? We play every week," said one of the guys.

"Well, I've never told anyone, but I'm a true hermaphrodite. I have a penis and a vagina. I've decided to go to the hospital on Monday and have my vagina sewn closed. I won't be able to play because of the stitches."

Everyone was quiet for a moment. Finally another guy spoke up and said, "Why don't you have your penis removed? Then you can hit from the red tees!"

• • •

347. A young executive fresh on the job was asked by his boss to take some out-of-town clients to lunch and then to play golf at the club. The young executive was thrilled. The foursome had a light lunch, played a quick eighteen holes, and went back to the clubhouse for a few beers before going home. He couldn't wait to get home and tell his wife the good news, but when he opened the front door he found his wife and boss making love on the sofa. He slammed the door, raced back to the club, went into the locker room, and started to put on his golf clothes. One of the attendants noticed him and said, "Say, I thought you golfed and went home already."

The young executive said, "Yeah, but when I got home I found my wife and my boss making love on the sofa. It looked like they were going to be there for a while, so I figured I had time to squeeze in another nine before nightfall."

• • •

348. A golf store owner was closing up shop one night when a lady came in. She said she had an awful argument with her husband and wanted to buy him something to show him she was sorry.

"You could get him a new Ping golf bag," said the store owner.

"No, I need something that says I'm a little more sorry than that," she responded.

"Well, then. How about a set of new graphite woods?" suggested the shop owner.

"Hmm. That's nice but I need something that really, really says I'm sorry," she insisted.

"I have just the thing," said the shop owner. "A brand-new fourteen-karat gold-plated putter. He'll be the envy of all his friends. It even comes with a place for an inscription."

"It's perfect! I'll take it," exclaimed the woman. "But what should I put on it?"

The shop owner jokingly quipped, "How about 'NEVER UP, NEVER IN'?"

The lady burst into laughter, saying, "That is exactly what we were fighting about!"

• • •

349. Two buddies were out playing a friendly game of golf on a Saturday. One of them was teeing off at the sixth hole when a beautiful naked lady ran past. Both men stared for as long as she was in sight. After she was gone, the first golfer set up for his shot again. Just as he was about to hit it, two men in white coats ran past. "What the heck's going on here?" the golfer said to his friend. He once again set up for his shot. Not taking any chances, he looked up before swinging. Sure enough, a third man went running by in a white coat, but this one was carrying two large buckets of sand. The golfer stopped the man and said, "What the heck's going on with you people? What's with the naked lady and what's with the sand?"

"Well, that lady is nuts and once a week somehow manages to escape from the asylum down the road. Her obsession is to strip naked and run across the golf course. The first two guys you saw were nurses. They're racing to see which one catches her and gets to carry her home like that."

"But what about you?" asked the golfer.

"Oh, I won last week. These buckets of sand are my handicap."

• • •

350. Four women were out on the golf course when one noticed a white blur approaching from a distance. As it came closer she pointed it out to her friends. Finally, they could see it was a streaker.

As the nude guy ran past the women, one remarked, "I think I know him. Wasn't that Dick Green?"

Another answered, "No, I think it was just the reflection off the grass."

• • •

351. One under par is a birdie and one over par is a bogey. And, of course, there's the "Lewinsky." That's where the shot lands three feet from the hole!

• • •

352. An old guy and a friend were golfing on the fifteenth hole, and it was obvious that the old guy's friend was having an off day. "Man, you're just not yourself today on the course. What's the matter?" asked the old guy.

"Well, I'm not sure, but I think my wife is dead," said the friend.

"What do you mean you *think* she's dead? Aren't you sure?" asked the old guy.

The friend explained, "The sex is the same but she doesn't say anything when I say I'm going golfing."

• • •

353. A guy goes to his doctor and complains that he hasn't felt well in a long time. The doctor can't find anything wrong with him so he orders a bunch of tests. About a week later, the guy is resting in bed when the doctor calls his wife with the results. "I'm not quite sure how to explain this," begins

the doctor. "I've consulted with two other doctors and they agree that the only way to keep your husband alive is to let him golf five times a week and give him all the sex he can handle." The woman thanks the doctor and hangs up the phone.

"What did the doctor say?" the man asked.

"I'm afraid it's pretty serious," his wife replied. The doctor says it's terminal."

• • •

354. A guy was setting up a tee shot on the fourth hole when an errant shot flew right at him and hit him in the crotch. He doubled over in excruciating pain, screaming for help. A doctor on the next hole came running over and examined him. The man finally caught his breath and told the doctor what happened. "Well, how bad is it?" asked the guy.

"I'm afraid it's bruised and pretty swollen. I'll have to put it in a splint for a week," said the doctor.

"You can't do that, Doc. I'm getting married in four days!" he exclaimed.

"That's your only option if you want it to heal normally," said the doctor. He then took four tongue depressors from his golf bag and made a little splint for the man's privates.

The wedding took place and the couple headed off to a hotel for their first experience together. The woman said, "I'm proud to tell you that I'm a virgin."

The man smiled and said, "So am I."

She said, "How can I be sure that you're a virgin?"

The man pulled off his clothes and said, "Look, it's still in the crate!"

• • •

355. Two guys were about to tee off on the sixth hole when a beautiful young lady wandered across their fairway seeming to be very confused. The first guy walked out to her and asked if he could help her.

"I hope so," she said. "I'm playing this course for the first time and I can't find the seventh hole."

The guy said, "We're one hole behind you on the sixth hole. You're on the seventh and your tee is right over there." She thanked the guy and headed to the seventh tee.

On the twelfth hole the young lady again wandered into their fairway. The same guy walked out and asked if he could help her. She said she was lost again.

The guy said, "We're still one hole behind you if you're on the thirteenth." He pointed it out to her and she thanked him.

Later, in the clubhouse, the guy saw the woman and offered to buy her a drink. He sat down and asked her what she did for a living. She said she was a gynecologist, to which the guy replied, "Then I'm still one hole behind you—I'm a proctologist!"

• • •

356. A beautiful, buxom blonde was playing a round of golf one day with a guy who had waited forever to date her to no avail. The guy was constantly distracted by her figure and was having a terrible game. He tried explaining that he was a much better golfer, but she knew he wasn't concentrating. On the twelfth hole he hit a wicked slice off the tee that hit a tree, bounced off a rock, and came back straight toward them. The ball took a couple of bounces and landed softly between her breasts.

As he approached her, she stopped him, saying, "Don't even think about it! You'll take the penalty!"

• • •

357. A golfer was sitting on a bench by the first tee, waiting for his partner to show up for their weekly round, when a beautiful, buxom redhead approached and uncovered her clubs. Ten minutes later the partner showed up to see his friend lying on the ground, unconscious and with a black eye.

"What the heck happened to you?" asked the partner, waking his friend.

"Do you see that beautiful redhead on the next fairway?"

His partner looked up. "Yeah, I see her."

"She came up to the first tee and uncovered her clubs. All I said was 'nice set'!"

• • •

358. A visiting Scotsman in full kilt dress was playing a qualifying round for the pro tournament. A beautiful lady in the gallery was smitten by his attire and flirtatiously asked, "Hey, Scotty. What do you wear under that kilt?"

"I dinna wear nothin'!" said the proud Scot.

"I don't believe you," said the woman.

"Well, stick your hand up there and find out," said Scotty.

She stuck her hand up his kilt and exclaimed, "My God, man. That's gruesome!"

"Well, stick your hand up there again, lassy. I think it *grew some* more!"

• • •

359. Two guys met up in the locker room after a round of golf one day. The first one said, "Hey, did you hear what happened to Bob on Sunday?"

"No, what happened?" asked the second.

"His round finished early, and when he went home he caught his wife in bed with another man," said the first.

The second guy turned white as a sheet and exclaimed, "Good thing he didn't end early on Saturday!"

• • •

360. A golfer drives over to the country club to play a round of golf after work one Friday. He's paired up with a beautiful redhead who turns out to be a pretty good golfer. After their round they go to the clubhouse for drinks and a bite to eat. They laugh all night and decide to spend the night together. They make passionate love all night, sleep most of the day Saturday, and do the same thing Saturday night. Sunday morning the woman wakes up and says, "Wow, what an incredible weekend. You're a fantastic lover. What's your secret, stud?"

"Nothing to it," he says. "It's just good course management!"

• • •

361. Two guys were finishing up their drinks near closing time at a local tavern near Pebble Beach. One looked over and saw a guy with a cigar in one hand, a huge drink in another, and no less than three beautiful girls falling all over him. "Hey, isn't that the reigning golf champion who's supposed to be defending his world title in about six hours?" asked the first guy.

"You know, I think you're right," said the second, smiling.

"What a waste," said the first. "He's getting tanked up and horny before a big match like that. He's got no sense of priority!"

"Ohh, I wouldn't say that!" said the second.

• • •

362. Q: Why is golf like playing with yourself?
    A: Because it's a lot of fun, but pretty gross for everyone else to watch!

• • •

363. A pro golfer married an auctioneer and they went on a two-week honeymoon to Florida to golf and have fun. The first night they shared incredibly satisfying romance and both went right to sleep afterward—he, of course dreaming of golf, and she dreaming of the ultimate estate sale. The next morning at breakfast, they noticed people kept staring at them or furtively turning away from them. They went to the desk clerk to see what the problem was.

"You mean, you don't know?" asked the desk clerk.

"No, I'm afraid we don't," said the golfer.

"The guests on your floor, plus all the guests one up and one down, heard you screaming in your sleep last night," said the clerk. "All night long it was 'FORE' and 'Can I get SIX,' 'FORE' and 'can I get SIX.' "

• • •

364. Some golf buddies were sitting in the local tavern discussing golf and women. All of the golfers were married or engaged, except for one. He was complaining to his mates about the dating scene. "You guys are lucky. I'll never find a woman who can love me *and* tolerate all the golf I play."

At that very moment a beautiful, shapely brunette walked in and sat down at the table across from them. He made eye contact with her a couple of times and was just dying to say hello. Egged on by his friends, the guy worked up enough courage to walk over and make conversation. Surprisingly, she asked him to join her. It was a match made in heaven. They laughed all night and were having such a good time that they didn't even realize it was closing time.

"Can I get your phone number?" he asked sheepishly.

"Better than that, why don't you just come over for a nightcap or two?" she said, smiling.

"That would be great," he said, "but I have to tell you, I'm a golf nut. In fact, I golf four times a week. It seems like every time I get into a relationship I get hurt because the women I'm with don't like golf."

"Believe me when I say you have nothing to worry about," she teased.

"How can I be sure?" he asked.

She leaned over to him, exposing a little more of herself, and purred, "Is that a graphite-shafted Big Bertha in your pocket, or are you glad to see me?"

• • •

365. Every Friday a fourth-grade teacher asked her class a near-impossible trivia question with the promise that whoever got the right answer could take the following Monday off with an A for the day. One Friday the teacher asked, "Okay, class, how many gallons of water in the Atlantic Ocean?" The kids just stared at her. The next week she asked, "All right, how many shovels of sand in the Sahara Desert?" No one responded. The week after that, the teacher was just about to ask her question when one of the kids dropped a bag of ball bearings. "All right, who's got balls of steel?"

Little Johnnie stood up and said, "Arnold Palmer! See ya next Tuesday, Teach!"

• • •

366. Four college-aged girls decided to work as caddies at a swanky golf resort in Florida between school terms. The resort hired a new pro midseason, so they all decided to play practical jokes on him.

"I rearranged his teaching charts so he didn't know who he was talking to at any given moment," said the first.

"Well, I replaced all his Ping clubs with thirty-year-old junk clubs I found in the storage shed," said the second.

"That's nothing," said the third. "I found a box of condoms in his desk drawer and put pinholes in all of them."

The fourth girl just fainted!

• • •

367. Two buddies met for a round of golf one day.

"Say, how goes it with you and your wife?" asked the first.

"Lousy," said the second. "After fifteen years of marriage, she's divorcing me, and all over an easy five-and-a-half footer I made on the eighteenth last weekend."

"She's divorcing you over a putt?" asked the first.

"It wasn't a putt. Her name was Sherry!"

• • •

368. A couple had a whirlwind, sixty-day romance and, even though they didn't know too much about each other, they decided to get married. Just before the wedding the husband said, "Honey, there is something I have to tell you. I'm a golf fanatic and I have to play every day."

"I also need to tell you something," she said. "I'm a hooker, and I need to do it every day."

"That's okay," he said, "we'll just play dogleg lefts."

• • •

369. Nine Rules for Bedroom Golf:

1. A player shall furnish his own equipment for play, normally one club and two balls.

2. Play on course must be approved by the owner of the hole.
3. For most effective play, the club should have a firm shaft. Course owners are permitted to check shaft stiffness before play begins.
4. Course owners reserve the right to restrict club length to avoid damage to the hole.
5. The object of the game is to take as many strokes as necessary until the course owner is satisfied that play is complete. Failure to do so may result in denial of permission to play again.
6. It is considered bad form to begin playing the hole immediately upon arrival. Experienced players will normally take time to admire the entire course, paying special attention to well-formed mounds and bunkers.
7. Players are cautioned not to mention other courses they have played or are currently playing to the owner of the course being played. Upset owners have been known to damage a player's equipment for this reason.
8. Slow play is encouraged; however, players should be prepared to proceed at a quicker pace at the owner's request.
9. It is considered an outstanding performance, time permitting, to play the same hole several times in one match.

• • •

370. A golf pro was giving lessons to a beautiful young woman one morning. He started to reach from behind her to show her the proper stance and swing when he noticed his fly was open. He quickly tried to zip it up but got it caught on her skirt in the process. Unable to get it loose, the two of them started walking toward the clubhouse to get a pair of pliers. Suddenly, a big black dog came out of the bushes. Yelling, "Payback's a bitch!" he threw a bucket of cold water on them.

• • •

371. A former porn star turned golfer once yelled "Fore" on the golf course and three dozen came running!

• • •

372. A foursome of young women was getting set to tee off on the fourth hole at their club when they heard a rustling sound. They couldn't figure out what it was or where it was coming from. One of the ladies went to search the area.

"Pssst," said the lady in a hushed tone. "Come over here, quickly."

The other ladies came rushing over to see what the commotion was. "Look," said the first lady. "Through the bushes over there. It's a guy going to the bathroom in public."

"Who is it?" asked another lady.

"I don't know," said the first. "His face is completely covered by the bush. But I can tell you he's not a member of *this* club!"

• • •

373. Golf and sex are two things you can do alone and still have fun doing it.

• • •

374. Two golfers were talking while playing at Garland one day. "So, how's the new romance going?" asked the first guy.

"I had to dump her," said the second. "She told me she golfed, but I found out she was lying."

"What did you do? Take her out for a round?" asked the first.

"No, it never got that far," said the second. "I knew she wasn't a golfer the first time we had sex and she didn't grab me with an interlocking grip."

• • •

375. Why golf is better than sex:
- It's legal to play golf professionally.
- The shafts are always firm.
- A golf round always last a few hours.

- Everyone cheers when you get it in the hole.
- You can count on it once a week in good weather.
- You can tell everyone about it afterward.

• • •

376. Four friends met for poker, cigars, and beer every Saturday afternoon. On one particular Saturday, one of the foursome called to say he couldn't make it because his neighbor was playing in a local golf tournament. The following Saturday he called and said the same thing. The next Saturday one of his friends called to ask if he was coming over.

"Sorry, I can't make it today. My neighbor is competing for the state championship," he said.

"Why all this sudden interest in watching your neighbor play golf?" asked the friend.

"Oh, I don't watch my neighbor. Whenever he's out golfing I make love to his wife!"

• • •

SHORT TAKES AND MORE

377. Two detectives are standing over a dead man named Juan. The first detective asks, "So, how do you think he was killed?"

The second one says, "Can't you tell? He was killed with a golf gun."

The first one says, "What the hell is a golf gun?"

The second one replies, "I don't know, but it sure made a hole in Juan."

• • •

378. A detective walks into the home of a couple where the woman lies dead on the floor with a 3-iron beside her head. The policeman looks at the husband and says, "You killed her, didn't you?" The husband replies, "Yes, I did." The detective says, "Looks like you hit her about eight times in the forehead with that three-iron." The husband says, "It was ten, but put me down for a five."

• • •

379. A blonde is out playing golf one beautiful sunny day, when she suddenly screams and runs back to the clubhouse. She approaches the club pro and says, "I've just been stung by a bee!"

"Where were you stung?" he asks.

"Between the first and second holes," she replies.

"I told you your stance was too wide!"

• • •

380. A bunch of businessmen are sitting at the bar discussing golf. One brags about shooting an eighty at Pebble, another boasts about shooting a hole in one at the Bear. Myron, the office nerd, stands up and says, "Oh yeah? Well, I once shot a seventy-six at Hilton Head. Of course, I got tired after three holes and went home!"

• • •

381. Have you heard about the celebrity golf tournament?
OJ had a wicked slice.
Heidi Fleiss kept hooking.
Ted Kennedy couldn't stay out of the water hazards.
Nobody dared to go into sudden death with Jack Kevorkian.
Greg Louganis kept wanting to putt the ball into the wrong hole.
John Bobbitt couldn't get the ball in the air.
Monica Lewinsky kept lipping the hole.

• • •

382. Two guys walk into their club without having scheduled a tee time in advance. The manager explains that there aren't any tee times available and that they'll have to schedule one in advance. The first guy says, "I'll bet if Arnold Palmer and Jack Nicklaus showed up you'd find a starting time for them."
The manager says, "Of course we would, sir. They're known professionals."
The second golfer says, "Well, I happen to know they're on tour and won't be coming, so we'll take their time."

• • •

383. A foursome of older women were taking their time teeing off at the tenth hole. Golfers were starting to back up. Just as they were about to play, a man rushed off the ninth green and screamed, "Excuse me, ladies. I need to play through. I've just heard that my wife has been taken seriously ill."

• • •

384. A couple stood at the altar waiting for the priest to marry them. The bride-to-be looked down and saw a set of golf clubs beside her fiancé's feet.

"What on earth are you doing with those golf clubs?" she whispered.

"This won't take all afternoon, will it?"

• • •

385. A violent thunderstorm quickly came over the golf course. An old golfer said to his partner, "Grab your one-iron and stand out in the rain!"

"What are you, nuts?" said the other golfer. "We'll get struck by lightning."

"Don't worry—not even God could hit a one-iron!"

• • •

386. Amateur: "How do I get better backspin on my shots?"

Pro: "Well, tell me. About how far do you hit a five-iron?"

Amateur: "About a hundred and thirty feet."

Pro: "A hundred and thirty feet? Why in hell would you want the ball to spin back?"

• • •

387. One day the golf pro at the local club walked into the clubhouse for a quick lunch before giving lessons. At the end of a bar sat a beautiful blonde all by herself. He immediately approached her and asked if she would like to play some golf. She turned to him and said, "I don't know anything about the game. Heck, I wouldn't even know how to hold the caddie!"

• • •

388. A Jew, a Catholic, and a Mormon were having a few drinks at the bar after an interfaith golf tournament. The Jew said, "I have four sons. One more and I'll have a basketball team."

The Catholic said, "Ah, that's nothing. I have ten sons. One more and I'll have a football team."

The Mormon looked at them both and said, "You guys

don't know anything. Why, I have seventeen wives. One more and I'll have a golf course!"

• • •

389. Upon graduating from college, a young man reports to the local golf course to start his first job. The greenskeeper meets him at the maintenance shed, leads him to the lawn-mower, and says to cut the back nine before noon. The young man protests and says, "Hey, I graduated with top honors from a respectable college. I can't cut the grass."

The greenskeeper says, "Oh, right, I forgot. Here, I'll show you how."

• • •

390. Feeling very proud after having walked around with her dad on the golf course for the first time, a little girl couldn't wait to tell everyone at the clubhouse about it. "My daddy is the best golfer in the whole world. He can play for hours and still keep the ball from hardly ever going into those little holes."

• • •

391. Lost ball theory: Every lost ball is found by someone, and no doubt kept by the person finding it, thus making it, in fact, a stolen ball. Therefore, the person losing the ball shouldn't compound the misdemeanor by charging himself a penalty stroke.

• • •

392. Two girlfriends talking on the phone: "I went golfing with John yesterday," says the first girl.

"Really? How does he handle the woods?" asks her friend.

"I wouldn't know," sighs the first girl. "He insisted on playing golf all day."

• • •

393. A single golfer was taking so much time with his tee shots that a crowd of foursomes had caught up and gathered behind him. Noticing the crowd's growing impatience the

guy said, "I have every right to take my time addressing my ball."

A few seconds went by and someone shouted, "Quick, someone tell him where the hell his ball lives so we can finish!"

• • •

394. A married golfer with an eye for the ladies was sitting in the clubhouse getting soused when a beautiful young lady walked by. He was considering asking her out but started thinking about the consequences and then began to mutter out loud. "It's just not worth it," he said. "It never goes as well as you hoped, it's expensive, and when I do it my wife gets angry."

A guy at the next table heard his ramblings and said, "Hey, look, pal, you knew full well what to expect when you took up golf!"

• • •

395. A guy walks into his boss's office and says he needs to leave for a few days to attend his grandmother's funeral out of town. The boss says, "Isn't this the third or fourth grandmother you've had die in as many years?"

"No, sir," assures the guy.

Knowing that the Masters is in town, the boss says, "I wish you cared about work as much as you do golf."

The guy bursts out laughing. "You're kidding, right? I could never take work *that* seriously!"

• • •

396. The hack golfer strolled onto the course for his usual tee time, much to the dismay of the caddie. On the fourth hole the hack golfer hit his ball into a huge bunker. "What club should I use to get out?" asked the hack.

The frustrated caddie, knowing that it would take at least an hour, said, "It doesn't matter. Just take plenty of food and water!"

• • •

397. A group of guys were at a sports bar one night discussing which sport was the best. Hockey and football seemed to be the two most talked about when one guy spoke up, "You're all wrong. Golf is definitely the best sport in the world."

"You're crazy," said one of the guys. "Golf is the most unnatural sport ever invented."

"What do you mean unnatural?" asked the second guy.

"There's something just not right about a game where the person with the most hits loses!"

• • •

398. Two guys were looking at the latest and most expensive set of clubs at the local pro shop. One of the guys picked up the set and said, "I think I'll buy these to help my wife with her constipation."

"How the heck is a new set of two-thousand-dollar golf clubs going to help your wife with her constipation?" asked the second guy.

"Are you kidding?" explained the first guy. "She's gonna shit her pants when she sees these!"

• • •

399. Two golf buddies arrived at the golf club about forty-five minutes early and decided to have a drink to loosen up and unwind from work before they played. Things got a little out of hand and they ended up getting plastered. They somehow managed to stumble out to the first tee with their clubs and tried unsuccessfully for the longest time to tee up their balls. A foursome of older women was watching the drunks and anxiously waiting to get started. Finally out of patience, one said, "You should be ashamed of yourselves. Such behavior in public is an embarrassment to everyone."

"Shay, you're right, old lady," said the first one, slurring his words. "I'm in no condishun to drive."

His friend hiccupped and said, "Drive! Hell, you're in no condishun to putt, neither."

• • •

400. Two older pro golfers were talking one day in the club-house. "I'm thinking about retiring, but I don't know what I'll do with myself," said the first pro.

"What do you mean?" said the second.

"Most people golf and fish when they retire. That's what I do now!"

• • •

401. A guy was enjoying a quick round of golf after work one day. While waiting to tee off on the fourth hole, he noticed that the guy teeing off in front of him had two caddies. After the guy was done with his shot the first guy remarked, "It must be nice to have two caddies. I can't even afford one."

"Oh, these," said the golfer. "My ex-wife complains that I don't spend enough time with the kids."

• • •

402. A business owner decides to take up golf so he can take clients out to the links and hopefully increase sales. He goes to the driving range, putting course, and municipal course every lunch hour and every night after work for two months straight, but he just can't seem to get the hang of it. A friend suggests he take some lessons, so he goes to the local golf club to sign up. He arrives for his first lesson, buys a bucket of balls, and puts a few down to warm up. About that time the pro walks out to the practice area. "Just a second," he says. "Before you go knocking balls around, let's start at the beginning by swinging the club without hitting anything."

"What the hell are you talking about?" says the businessman angrily. "That's why I'm here to begin with!"

• • •

403. Q: What's the worst foursome to play behind and why?

A: Monica Lewinsky, OJ Simpson, Ted Kennedy, and Bill Clinton. Monica is a hooker, OJ is a slicer, Kennedy can't drive over water, and Clinton doesn't know which hole to play.

• • •

404. Two friends were talking about their financial portfolios while golfing one day. "My investments don't seem to be doing very well," said the first golfer. "I called my broker to ask him how it was going."

"Really? What did he say?" asked the second golfer.

"He said he broke eighty that morning," said the first golfer. "I wasn't sure if he was referring to his golf score or investors, so I fired him!"

• • •

405. A golfer and his teenage son were out on the links one day. The father was teaching the son how to play. "Remember," said the father, "one of the most polite things you can do on the course is to keep your game moving along. Avoid slow play at all costs. If not, you could get a penalty." He repeated this a few times during the day.

While waiting for a slow foursome to finish teeing off on the fourteenth hole, the father again reminded his son about quick play. Just then a black cloud formed over the foursome and a bolt of lightning struck two feet away from them. The shock sent the foursome hurtling forty yards down the fairway. The son turned to his dad and exclaimed, "I see what you mean!"

• • •

406. First golfer: "It seems a certain Scotsman had been playing golf with the same ball for over fifteen years when he abruptly quit playing altogether."

Second golfer: "What happened?"

First golfer: "One day he hit a bad tee shot that soared off deep into the woods. He looked for more than three hours but never found it, so he quit!"

• • •

407. The on-duty nurse in the emergency room at the local hospital took a call from a middle-aged man in a crisis. She stopped a doctor between patients to ask him for advice. "I have a forty-two-year-old man on the phone complaining of nausea, a racing heart, jittery limbs, and the inability to concentrate. He wants to know if he should call an ambulance.

What should I tell him?"

"Tell him to go out and take up golf," said the doctor.

There was a brief pause while the nurse spoke to the man. "He says he just played thirty-six holes," said the nurse.

"Ah, there's the problem," said the doctor. "Tell him to quit!"

• • •

408. Two golfers were playing a round of golf in Florida. The first golfer went off to find his ball in the rough while the second one drove the cart to the fairway. After five minutes the second golfer went to look for his friend. He found him buried up to his waist in quicksand and sinking fast. "Don't move a muscle!" shouted the second golfer. "I'll go and get a rope to pull you out."

"Forget that!" said the first. "Bring me a sand wedge!"

• • •

409. A group of snobs were sitting at their usual table in the clubhouse enjoying Cuban cigars and fine cognac after a round of golf one day. One of the snobs looked around the room and said, "Gosh, what *is* this club coming to? Just look at the caliber of people in here today. I say, you must agree that there's really nothing more important than good breeding."

A guy smoking a White Owl at the next table leaned over and said, "Good breeding is fine, but I also like to get in a little golf now and then!"

• • •

410. Funny thing about hack golfers: After hitting a bad shot they either cuss, look at the club as if it were damaged, gesture at some nonexistent thing that distracted them, say the sun was in their eyes, or blame the caddie for giving them the wrong club. But if they are lucky enough to hit a decent shot, the hollering is louder than thunder, the ego bigger than the course, and the stride is much quicker. That is, of course, 'til the next hole!

• • •

411. Two friends met at the local watering hole for a quick drink or two at lunch. "What's the matter?" asked the first guy. "You look depressed today."

"Oh, I just got back from a doctor's appointment and the doctor's mad at me," said the second.

"How come?" asked the first.

"He told me a month ago I needed to lose weight, so I took up golf."

"So, how's it going?" asked the first.

"Terrible. Between the beer carts, snack stands, cigars, and driving a cart, I gained twelve pounds!"

• • •

412. The course landscaper kept finding litter and empty bottles in sand traps. Each day a different trap would be full of junk. He knew it had to happen after the course closed because he personally cleaned each trap every night. One day he arrived at the club extra early and set out with a cart to see what was going on. Sure enough, in the thirteenth hole bunker, there slept a homeless man near a pile of litter.

"Say, what the heck do you think you're doing in there? You can't sleep in these sand traps," said the landscaper. "Get out of there right now, and don't let me catch you on this course again!"

The guy got up, dusted himself off, and said, "Well, this is no way to attract new members! I'll take my business elsewhere."

• • •

413. A foursome of Asian businessmen were teeing off at Pebble Beach one morning. One of the men was complaining about the caddie assigned to him.

"What's wrong with your caddie?" asked one of the men. "You had him last week and he seemed okay to us."

"Oh, really?" he retorted. "Then it must be my accent. Every time I ask for a sand wedge he brings me corned beef on rye!"

• • •

414. An avid golf viewer decided to take up the sport. Since his neighbor played every Sunday morning he asked if he could tag along one time and learn some things. The neighbor was more than happy to teach him the game. So, the guy spent a bunch of money on equipment and was eagerly waiting his first day on the course. The neighbor told him all the techniques and warned him not to expect too much his first time out. Despite all that, the guy was hitting excellent tee shots, getting to the green easily, and putting with ease. By the ninth hole the guy was actually ahead of his neighbor. "I thought you said this was your first time out!" snapped the neighbor angrily. "How are you doing this?"

"I don't know," said the guy. "I just close my eyes before each shot, and take a swing."

"Aha!" cried the exasperated neighbor. "THIS time, you have to leave your eyes open!"

• • •

415. A fifty-five-year-old man had wanted all his life to take his wife golfing at St. Andrews in Scotland. The kids were on their own and the house was paid for, so he decided that this was to be the year. He bought two first-class tickets, brand-new his-and-her golf attire, and made reservations at the course. When they arrived for their game, they were dismayed to learn that there would be a thirty-minute delay due to a ceremony at the first green. Curious, they headed out to see what it was about. When they got there, they saw people dressed in black with sad looks on their faces.

The husband leaned over to someone in the crowd and asked, "Say, what's going on?"

"Ach, they're all mourning the loss of Shamos," said the guy.

"What happened?" asked the husband.

"Ach, after thirty-two years of playing golf, he lost his ball. He looked for three days straight and died of exposure!"

• • •

416. Every week a guy goes out to golf and every week he comes home crabbing and moaning about his poor play. One particular week he came home, threw his clubs all over the garage, cut his bag in half, and burned his golf shoes. Finally fed up, his wife scolded him, saying, "If it's that bad, why don't you just give up the damned game!"

"What, and give up my only form of relaxation?"

• • •

417. An excellent golfer and a hack were paired in their club's annual hi-lo Spring Fling tournament, with the top prize being five thousand dollars. While waiting to tee off at the first hole, the good golfer turned to the hack and said, "Given your handicap, it looks like I'll have to shoot in the low seventies for us to win."

"What will I have to shoot for us to win?" asked the hack.

"Probably the other golfers!"

• • •

418. An English literature professor being interviewed by the BBC was describing his lifelong pursuit of learning golf:
   • It was the best of times, it was the worst of times . . .
   • Putting is such sweet sorrow . . .

- It is better to have golfed and lost, than never to have golfed at all . . .
- Two-iron, or not two-iron, that is the question . . .

• • •

419. Two friends met at the local club for a round of golf. One was a writer, the other a teacher. "Say, whatever happened to that book on golf terms you were writing?" asked the teacher.

"Oh, that," replied the writer. "I sent it to the publisher but it was rejected."

"Why is that?" asked the teacher.

"After I removed all the cuss words it was only four pages long!"

• • •

420. Two guys were heading to the clubhouse after playing the eighteenth when they happened upon a Scotsman sitting near a rough, crying like a baby. His golf buddy was trying to console him.

"There, there, Haggis. It'll be all right. It's not the end of the world, ya know," said the Scot's buddy.

"What's wrong with him?" asked one of the golfers.

"Ach, he lost his ball and canna find it," said the buddy.

The guys felt sorry for the man and went off into the rough to look for the man's ball. After a minute or so they couldn't find it so they decided to give him one of their balls and pretend they had found his.

The Scotsman, still sobbing, thanked the two men. When the golfers were gone, the Scot's buddy looked at the ball and exclaimed, "Wait a minute, laddie, that's not your ball!"

The Scotsman smiled and said, "Works every time!"

• • •

421. Comments heard on the course from golfers in different professions:
  - Garbage hauler hitting a fairway shot over the green: " 'Mon back, 'mon back."

- A dentist setting up for a twenty-foot putt: "Open just a little wider, please."
- A president talking to the club ranger: "I did not hit that ball, Top Flight III, through the clubhouse window. I never saw that ball."
- A bandleader talking about his golf score: "A five, six, seven, eight ..."
- An IRS agent in the rough: "What do you mean I'm being penalized?"
- A sports announcer on his first fairway shot: "It's a long drive to center field, it's hooking, hooking ... foul ball!"
- A veterinarian on a long par-3 left: "I hate doglegs."
- A butcher watching his tee shot go wildly off to the right: "It figures!"

• • •

422. An out-of-town golfer stopped by the local municipal course to squeeze in a round before a big afternoon meeting. He got a tee time but was told there were no caddies available and carts weren't permitted. The caddie master did say, however, that there was an experimental program being tested at the golf course using robot caddies. After being reassured that the robotic caddie was actually quite good, the man agreed to use one.

When the guy returned with the robot, he was all smiles. "This thing is great," said the golfer. "Every club call-out was correct, all the yardages were perfect to an inch, and he didn't smart off once. I played the game of my life!"

"Yeah, everyone likes the robots," said the caddie master. "Unfortunately, we're going to have to cancel the program because the robots give off too much glare, which distracts other golfers."

"Why not simply put them in caddie uniforms?" suggested the golfer.

"We tried that last month, but they formed a union and went on strike!"

• • •

423. Golfing student: "So, how am I doing after just six lessons?"
Club pro: "Very well."
Golfing student: "You mean my game is improving?"
Club pro: "Oh, no. Your game stinks, but you're throwing the clubs as far as guys who have been playing for years!"

• • •

424. The president of a posh country club was interviewing prospective new members one afternoon. About every ten minutes the president would excuse himself, open the window, and yell, "Green side up!" This went on for nearly an hour.

Finally, in exasperation, the prospective member asked, "Why do you keep shouting 'green side up' out the window?"

"I needed some resodding work done immediately in time for a big tournament this weekend," said the president. "The only company that was available consists of all blonde females!"

• • •

425. Two axioms to follow when participating in company golf outings:
1. The boss always wins.
2. If the boss is behind, refer to axiom number one.

• • •

426. The latest craze on the pro golf circuit was a set of twins named Juan and Amal. They were breaking and setting new club records throughout the tour. They played alike, dressed alike, and ate the same foods. Well, one day the top photographer from a big sports magazine wanted to take a picture of each of them and place them side by side in the magazine. The deal was, if anyone could guess which one was which, he would have a chance to win an all-expenses-paid trip to Pebble Beach for golf and lunch with the twins. Juan showed up for the shoot on time, but Amal was nowhere in sight. The photographer was getting more and more angry as the time grew late.

Finally, the twin's manager said, "Look, these guys look exactly the same. Why not just use two photos of Juan? After all, if you've seen Juan, you've seen Amal."

• • •

427. Two executives were playing on the local course, discussing their game and their careers. "I played golf with my boss the other day," said the first. "We went into the eighteenth tied. I hit a perfect shot that landed in a direct line to the green. My boss topped his shot leaving him about 275 yards to the hole."

"What happened then?" asked the second.

"Are you kidding? I'm trying to make VP: I conceded the putt!"

• • •

428. Two out-of-shape executives were told by the company physician to lose some weight before they became high risks for a stroke. They decided to take up golf. As they approached the first tee the first guy said, "You know anything about golf?"

"Not a damned thing," said the second. "But it looks easy on TV."

"Well, with us being so out of shape, I doubt we'll last very long."

"I agree," said the second. "Let's say we play until one of us gets a hole in one, then head to the clubhouse for a few beers!"

• • •

429. A man came home from the golf course and promptly threw his clubs into the trash, cussing the whole time.

"If you really hate the game so much, why do you play each week?" his wife inquired.

"It's not *the* game of golf that bothers me," said the husband. "It's *my* game of golf!"

• • •

430. An avid golfer was paired with the local hack for a round of golf. By the tenth hole, the avid golfer had had enough and started to head back to the clubhouse. "Hey, just where do ya think you're going?" asked the hack.

"I can't play with you," said the avid golfer. "All you do is complain. On the first nine holes you complain it takes you too long to putt out. Then on the tenth hole you get a hole in one and have the nerve to complain that you got cheated out of putting!"

• • •

431. Two women met in the supermarket one afternoon. "Say, how's your husband's golf game?" asked the first.

"I'm not quite sure," said the second.

"Why not ask him?" said the first.

"Well, when he comes home smiling, I assume it was a good day. When he comes home with wet shoes, dirty knees, and twigs in his hair, I don't ask."

• • •

432. Having forgotten which of two golf courses his foursome was sneaking off to one day, a guy called his friend's office and asked, "Where's David?"

"Oh, he stepped away for a while," said the secretary in a slight whisper.

"That much I know," said the man. "But did he step away ten miles or twenty?"

• • •

433. A guy returns home from having played eighteen holes and is beaten up pretty badly.

"What the hell happened to you?" asks his wife.

"It was my day to keep score!"

• • •

434. Four guys from the same company decided to play a round of golf after work with the loser having to buy dinner and drinks. It seemed the darker it got, the further behind one of the golfers was. Finally the other three golfers started to complain.

"Why don't you just give it up already! It's dark and we're all hungry."

"No way am I giving up," said the first. "Now, shut up and hold those damn flashlights still!"

• • •

435. Golfer: "Would you mind wading into the pond and retrieving my ball?"
Caddie: "What?"
Golfer: "It's my lucky ball."
Caddie: "What are you, a Scot?"

• • •

436. Your first golf shot of the day is never made to order,
Rarely down the middle, usually in the water.
Your second slices in the woods—a place no man dare tread,
Your gutsy third comes whizzing back, almost taking off your head,
You chip your fourth back into play,
Your fifth lands in the beach,
Your sixth sprays sand but it's still there,
Your seventh just might reach,
Oh, well, two putts for eight; it happens now and then.
Oh, no! My ninth just rimmed the cup. Oh, God! I took a ten!

• • •

437. Two friends met up for a round of golf one day. One looked at the other and said, "Say, have you been losing weight?"
"Yeah, I'm on the Arnold Palmer diet," said the other.
"Really, what's that?" asked the first.
"You live on greens all summer."

• • •

438. A guy driving to work one Friday noticed a brand-new golf club had opened up in a posh section of town. He stopped there after work and tried to walk into the clubhouse, but was stopped by the doorman. "Sorry, young man, but you have to have proper attire to enter—you must wear some sort of a tie."

So, the guy went back out to his car and looked around in the trunk for anything at all that could pass for a tie. All he could find was a small set of jumper cables. He fashioned them in a crude bow tie around his neck, walked back up to the doorman, and asked, "Is this okay?"

The doorman looked at him kind of funny and said, "Well . . . yeah, I guess, but don't try and start anything."

• • •

439. A golf nut went to a used car lot and bought a 1996 Lincoln Town Car in mint condition. The only problem with the car was that it had an Arnold Palmer sticker on the back bumper. He drove the car home, peeled off the Palmer sticker, and replaced it with a sticker with John Daly's name on it. Now he claims the car drives better and goes farther on a tank of gas.

• • •

440. A well-to-do golfer in Mississippi belonged to a posh country club. He had his own personal parking space and owned a personalized, deluxe golf cart complete with weather protection and a roof. One day a golf ball landed on the top of the roof and cracked a hole in it, permitting water to come inside on rainy days. The golfer drove the cart to the pro shop and asked that one of the maintenance men fix the leak.

Three weeks passed and the golfer still hadn't received his golf cart. He found the maintenance man and demanded, "Where the heck is my golf cart? How come it isn't fixed yet?"

The repairman looked at him blankly and, in a southern drawl, said, "Well, buddy, it's like this. When it's a-raining I cain't fix it, and when the sun shines, it don't leak!"

• • •

441. Two elderly female golfers were resting on a bench after the first nine one Saturday when suddenly a male streaker ran past. One lady had a stroke . . . the other couldn't reach.

• • •

442. Someone once said that there's nothing like a peaceful game of golf to quiet your nerves, build your muscles, and strengthen your resolve . . . just in case you ever decide to play again.

• • •

TEE SHOTS

---

443. For twenty years four old friends had been playing golf every Sunday morning promptly at 8:15. One Sunday morning they noticed a guy patiently watching and waiting as they teed off. At every tee he seemed to catch up to them and wait. As they got to the fourth tee, the guy walked up to the foursome and handed them a handwritten card. The card read, "I am deaf and mute. May I play through your group this morning?" The players were enraged by the gesture and told the guy that nobody was playing through them and that he had just better get used to staying behind them.

Two holes later, one of the foursome was in the fairway preparing to hit his second shot. As he was addressing the ball, he was suddenly struck in the back of the head with tremendous force by a golf ball, which sent him to his knees in agony. After a few seconds the player regained his balance and looked back up to the tee.

There stood the deaf-mute, waving his arm in the air, holding up four fingers.

• • •

444. Two friends are teeing off on a foggy, rainy par-3. They can see the flag, but not the green. The first golfer hits his ball into the fog toward the flag, and the second golfer does the same. They ride to the green to find their balls.

When they get there, they see that one ball is about six feet from the cup and the other is in the cup for a hole in one. Both were playing Top-Flite 2 balls so they couldn't determine which ball was which. They decide to ask the course ranger to decide.

After congratulating both golfers on fine shots in bad weather, the ranger asks, "Which one of you is playing the orange ball?"

• • •

445. A businessman decided to take up the game of golf so he could golf with his clients. He had never played before, so he bought a good set of clubs and signed up for lessons with the local club pro. The pro showed him the proper stance and swing, then said, "Just hit the ball toward the flag on the first green."

The businessman teed up and whacked the ball straight down the fairway and up onto the green, where it stopped inches from the hole. The pro was speechless.

"Now what?" asked the businessman.

"Uh, well, you're supposed to hit the ball into the cup."

"Oh, great! *Now* you tell me!"

• • •

446. A young man is paired up with a priest from a local parish. At a par-3 hole the priest asks, "What are you going to use on this hole, son?"

The young man says, "I think I'll use an eight-iron, Father. How about you?"

The priest says, "I'm going to hit a soft seven and pray."

The young man hits a beautiful 8-iron shot and puts the ball on the green. The priest tops his 7-iron shot and dribbles the ball out a few yards.

The young man says, "I don't know about you, Father, but in my church we keep our head down when we pray. "

• • •

447. A grandfather took his eighteen-year-old grandson to play golf at his country club. On a severely doglegged par-5, the

grandfather told his grandson, "You know, when I was about your age, my father taught me to aim right over those trees and I hit the green every time."

The grandson, thrilled at his grandfather's advice, thought about the comment and decided to give it a try. He hit a perfect drive, but it landed right in the middle of the fifty-foot trees.

The grandson looked angrily at the grandfather, who shrugged and said, "Of course, when I was your age, those trees were only twelve feet tall."

• • •

448. A newlywed couple decided to spend their honeymoon at an elegant golf resort they had heard about from some friends. The groom had made all the reservations and couldn't believe the rooms only cost $20 per night. When they arrived, they were stunned with the beauty of the grounds, the country club, and ther accommodations. They went to the resort's fine restaurant and had lobster and steak, with all the trimmings, and two bottles of champagne. The bill was only $12. They were shocked! They went to the lounge and danced and drank until 2 A.M. and it only cost $4. They were elated.

The next morning they decided to get up early and play a quick round of golf. For eighteen holes, a cart, and club rental, it only cost $10 for both of them. The salesman behind the counter handed each of them two golf balls and said, "Whatever you do, don't lose these golf balls."

"Sure thing," said the guy. "We're pretty good golfers."

Well, it happened that the guy lost one ball when he sliced his tee shot on the third hole and the woman lost one when she hooked her tee shot on the seventeenth hole. When they returned to the pro shop the salesman asked, "So, how did you do?"

The groom replied, "We did okay for our first time on this course, but we lost two of the golf balls you gave us."

The man behind the counter shook his head and said, "That will be four hundred dollars for the lost balls."

The groom was in shock. "Four hundred dollars! Where do you get off charging four hundred dollars for two golf balls?"

The manager heard the commotion and came over to see what was wrong. "What seems to be the problem here, sir?"

"What's the problem?" shouted the groom. "You charge twelve dollars for steak and lobster, four dollars for dancing and drinks, and twenty dollars for a night's stay. Now you want to charge us four hundred dollars for losing two balls?"

The manager replied, "You don't understand, sir; some hotels get you by the rent. Here . . ."

• • •

449. A golfer was getting set to hit his ball from about two feet in front of the tee markers on the first hole, right in front of the clubhouse. He approached the ball, concentrated, and was ready to swing when the starter said, "Excuse me, sir, you have to tee your ball from behind the tee markers for your first shot."

The man ignored the starter and continued to prepare for his shot. Just as he was ready to swing at the ball, the starter shouted, "I said, you have to tee your ball from behind the tee markers for your first shot—club rules."

The golfer angrily looked up at the starter and screamed, "This is my *second* shot, you moron!"

• • •

450. A magic genie was playing a round of golf one day and belted his fourth tee shot right down the middle of the fairway. Unfortunately, the ball bounced off the head of another golfer. The genie rushed down the fairway, helped the golfer up, and said, "Since I have hit you in the head with my ball, I will grant you one wish. What would you like?"

The golfer thought for a moment and said, "Well, I've always wanted to go to Hawaii and golf, but I am afraid to fly and I don't like the ocean. Can you make it possible for me to drive there?"

The genie replied, "I am so sorry. That would take far too long. Do you have a request for something a little easier?"

The golfer thought again. "Well, I have always wanted to understand women."

The genie paused for a moment and said, "Would that road be two lanes or four?"

• • •

451. A man wanted to fit in with the golfing crowd at work, so he bought a new set of clubs and asked one of his friends to show him how to use his clubs at the local driving range. They bought a couple of buckets and headed out to the tees. Over and over again the guy tried to get a solid hit but kept flubbing the ball, sending it only a few yards in front of the tees. The guy was getting angrier and angrier with each shot.

On his last ball he declared, "Stand back. I'm going to knock the damn cover off this ball." He reared back and with all his might hit the ball, sending it flying wildly off the tee. About that time a pigeon happened to fly into the ball's path and was killed instantly.

The guy's friend said, "Hey, look, your first birdie!"

• • •

452. A man was preparing for his tee shot on the fourth hole near some trees and not too far from the highway. He shanked his shot, sending it wildly slicing off into the trees and who knows where. He teed up another ball and forgot about it. About thirty minutes later a highway patrolman and the club pro approached him.

"Is this your ball, mister?" asked the policeman.

"It looks like mine," said the golfer.

"Do you have any idea what happened to the shot you hit?" demanded the officer. "It sailed through the trees, careened off the roof of a car, and crashed through the windshield of an oncoming tour bus. The two vehicles collided and both rolled down an embankment. There were no survivors."

"My gosh, I'm awfully sorry," said the golfer. "Is there anything I can do?"

The officer replied, "You might try keeping your left arm a little straighter and start your downswing more with your hips."

• • •

453. A hack golfer was setting up his tee shot at the first hole. He took numerous swings, throwing big chunks of grass in the air and missing the ball with every stroke. He turned to his caddie and jokingly said, "Looks like I have the worms running scared now."

The caddie quipped, "No doubt they're all hiding under the ball. That seems to be the safest place around!"

• • •

454. Two golfers were having a very frustrating day on the golf course. Both kept blowing par putts and hitting tee shots into the woods. One golfer was down to his last golf ball on the fourteenth hole. He hit a wicked slice into some nearby trees, so he and his partner trudged into the woods to find the ball. In the trees they noticed an old lady standing there watching them.

After about fifteen minutes of observation the old lady said, "Excuse me, mister, but is it cheating if I tell you where your ball is?"

• • •

455. A guy has a big match with a friend at his country club and wants to win in the worst way. He goes into the pro shop in search of a new driver. The club pro suggests a Great Big Bertha. After the match he returns to the pro shop to speak to the pro. "So, how'd you do with the Great Big Bertha?" asks the pro.

"Great," says the golfer. "I lost the match but I can throw these clubs forty yards farther than my old clubs!"

• • •

456. Two golfers were paired by the club ranger one day to keep up the speed of play. One of the golfers was fair, the other poor. The poor golfer said, "Say, let's make it interesting

and bet fifty dollars per drive. The longest drive on each hole wins." The fair golfer thought this guy had to be nuts and quickly agreed. On the next hole the fair golfer won easily. On the hole after, it was about dead even. The poor golfer went on to beat the fair golfer on the next four holes. Aware that the fair golfer was getting frustrated, the poor golfer shrugged modestly and said, "Gee. Somebody up there must like me."

Figuring out that he was being hustled, the fair golfer replied, "That's good, because if I lose the next hole, you're going to meet him soon!"

• • •

457. Two golfers were out playing a quick round one Wednesday after work. The first golfer kept hitting poor tee shots and complaining about it. "Man, if I only had a longer club, I could hit better tee shots." By the ninth hole his friend was getting tired of hearing the guy whine and complain about his game.

"Stop complaining!" shouted the second guy. "The only thing you'd accomplish by having a longer club is being able to create a bigger breeze when you whiff your shots!"

• • •

458. A twosome was just teeing off at the public course one afternoon. The first golfer stepped up, addressed the ball, and smacked a wicked slice that headed toward the next fairway. Seeing that the ball was headed right for a group of players, the golfer yelled out, "Fore!" Too late. The ball whacked another golfer right in the forehead. The first golfer ran over and apologized again and again.

"You idiot. That shot could've killed me!" said the dazed man.

"Hey, I said I was sorry, and I did yell fore," said the first golfer.

"Next time try yelling five," said the second.

"What does five mean?" asked the first golfer, puzzled.

Punching the man in the chin, he said, "It means you're gonna get hit!"

• • •

459. After shanking his tee shot into some thick woods, a hack golfer was assessing his second shot. "I have to somehow get this shot through these trees, past a pond, and over a bunker, then have it land on the green—close to the cup—if I'm going to make par," he said to his caddie. "What do you suggest?"

"How about a Bible!"

• • •

460. Two friends met for a round of golf at the municipal course one day after work. When they teed off on the fourth hole, a par-3, both shots landed near some trees. They walked over to where their balls were and waited for the foursome in front of them to finish putting out. Just then a golf ball came flying through the trees, knocking down branches and nearly striking one of the golfers. They turned around and saw another foursome by the third tee. The two friends finally putted out on the fourth and waited for the foursome behind them to get to the green.

"Say, fella," said one golfer angrily. "You nearly hit me with your tee shot. You should be more careful!"

"Hey, pal," said one of the golfers. "I just didn't have time to yell fore, okay?"

"Oh, really? You sure had plenty of time to yell 'Damn!'"

• • •

461. A hack golfer spent four hours and countless golf balls just getting through the twelfth hole. He teed up his ball on the thirteenth, took a mighty swing, and sent it wildly off into some woods. He turned to his caddie to ask if he saw where it landed, only to find the young man watching a beautiful woman on the next fairway. "What are you doing?" screamed the angry golfer. "You're supposed to be watching where my ball went!"

"Sorry, sir. I didn't expect you to hit it on the first swing."

• • •

462. A guy decided he wanted to learn to play golf so he could join a league with his neighbors. "Hey, how tough could it be?" he thought to himself. Not wanting to look bad, he went to the local golf store and spent over five thousand dollars on new golf clothes, deluxe clubs, the latest bag, and an assortment of golf gadgets and goodies. The next day he went to the local club to play his first game ever. He hired a caddie and approached the first tee. He reached into his golf bag, pulled out a new tee and expensive golf ball, and tried to stick the tree in the ground. As soon as he let go, the ball fell off the tee. He tried a second and third time, but with no luck. Finally, he got the ball to stay on the tee. Just then, a big gust of wind came and blew it off. The guy picked up his tee and ball, put them back in his bag, and headed for the clubhouse. "Hey, where are you going?" asked the confused caddie.

"Forget it," said the man. "I never thought it would be this tough!"

• • •

463. Two decent golfers were playing a competitive match one morning. After the ninth hole they decided to check their scores.

"Hey, you cheater!" said the first golfer. "Where do you get off saying you only took four strokes on the ninth hole? I saw you take five."

"Oh, no, you didn't," said the second golfer. "My first swing was just a practice swing."

"Oh, really?" said the first. "Well, if it was a practice swing, why did I hear you yell 'Shit'?"

• • •

464. A husband and wife were on the fairway on the tenth hole getting ready for their next shot when, out of nowhere, a tee shot from the next hole came straight at them, barely missing the husband's head. A few minutes later a woman appeared and started looking for her ball.

"Excuse me!" snapped the wife. "Are you nuts? Don't you know it's common courtesy to yell 'fore' when you hit a bad shot like that?"

"You're absolutely right," said the second. "I'm awfully

sorry. That's my husband standing over there. Why not tee up from here and take a shot at mine?"

• • •

465. Two friends met up one day at the local watering hole. One mentioned, "Say, my wife and I just got back from a four-day trip to the best golf resort in the region."

"Was it nice?" asked the second.

"Nice?" said the first. "They served us breakfast in bed, gave us champagne at night, and they had six beautiful courses."

"How did you decide which course to play on?" asked the second.

"Simple," said the first. "In the morning I would go outside my cabin door, tee up a ball, and take a mighty whack. Wherever it landed, that's the course we played!"

• • •

466. A golfer was teeing off with a few friends at a nice course in the country. His first tee shot of the day sliced way over near a henhouse, killing a farmer's prize-winning hen. The guy felt terrible and raced over to talk to the farmer.

"Gee, I'm sorry, mister," said the golfer. "Please let me replace her."

"Well, okay, but if you start laying eggs, I'm gonna sell you off to the traveling freak show that's in town!"

• • •

467. A female golfer was out on the course one day and shanked her tee shot deep into the woods. While out to find it, she came across an old shiny oil lamp. She started to rub the dirt away from it when a genie appeared.

"For freeing me from the lamp, I will grant you three wishes," said the genie. "But, be careful what you wish for, because your ex-husband will receive twice as much as you."

The lady thought for a moment. "For my first wish, I'll take a million dollars, and for my second wish I'd like to be the world's best golfer."

"Granted," said the genie. "What is your third wish?"

She thought for another moment. "Take away half my sex life."

• • •

468. A waiter was setting tables in the grillroom overlooking the course when suddenly a golf ball came flying through the window, shattering the pane and knocking over three glasses. A few minutes later a big burly guy came in and said, "I just hit a tee shot in here. Is this room considered in play?"

• • •

469. Two friends are playing at the local club one day. On the fourth hole the first golfer hits a wicked tee shot that slices into the adjoining fairway. The ball hits another player right between the eyes and knocks him unconscious. The golfers rush over to where the man is on the ground and notice that the ball is lying right between his legs. The first golfer screams, "Oh, my God, what should I do?"

The second golfer says, "Don't touch him. If you leave him there he becomes an obstruction and, according to the rules, you're allowed a drop two club-lengths away."

• • •

470. A deaf-mute is about to tee off on the first hole of a municipal golf course when a large burly guy yells, "Hey, you! Nobody tees off ahead of me."

Being deaf, the guy continues to prepare for his shot. Thinking the deaf-mute is ignoring him, the big guy runs up and knocks the poor guy to the ground, kicks his ball away, and prepares for his own shot.

After the big guy hits the ball and proceeds down the fairway, the mute gets up, brushes himself off, waits a moment, and again prepares his shot.

The deaf-mute then hits a beautiful shot straight up the middle of the fairway, striking the big guy in the back of the head and knocking him unconscious. The mute then walks down the fairway, rolls the big guy over, and holds up four fingers in front of his face.

• • •

165

471. A golfer took off an afternoon from work to play a round of golf. When he arrived at the club he found out that all the caddies were busy finishing up a mixed scramble.

"We don't have any caddies available right now, but we do have a Great Dane that's trained to carry clubs and retrieve balls," said the club pro.

Not wanting to carry clubs in the heat of summer, the golfer reluctantly agreed to use the Great Dane. To his surprise, the dog knew exactly where every tee shot landed. At the thirteenth tee two golfers carrying their bags happened by and said, "Hey, that guy's pretty smart using a dog for a caddie."

"Oh, he's not so smart," quipped the dog. "I still have to find his balls and tell him which club to use."

• • •

GOLFING AND WIVES

472. A man and his wife were golfing one day at a beautiful course near the countryside. On the fifth hole the man hooked his tee shot. It landed behind a huge old barn, which was blocking the way to the green. As he prepared his chip shot to the fairway, his wife said, "Wait, I have an idea. If I open the doors on both sides you can hit a low shot right through the barn and reach the green."

The man hit the ball perfectly through the barn doors, but unfortunately it hit his wife in the middle of the forehead and almost killed her. The man was so upset that he didn't play golf again for thirty years. One day his wife and friends finally convinced him to play again. They returned to the same course and, as luck would have it, on the fifth hole the man's tee shot landed in virtually the exact same spot. As he prepared for his chip shot back to the fairway, his friend said, "If you open these doors, you can hit a low shot through the barn and reach the green."

"No way!" said the guy. "The last time I tried that, I took nine on the hole."

• • •

473. A champion woman golfer was playing in a mixed foursomes event with her husband. On a short par-4, she hit a long drive that stopped four feet short of the front edge of the green. Her husband stepped up and flubbed the chip shot, sending it only about a foot. She shook her head, took out a 9-iron, and hit a perfect chip that stopped four inches from the cup. He stepped up for the putt but somehow screwed it up. She glared at him, tapped it in for five, and stormed off the green, barely able to contain her anger.

As they walked to the next tee, she fumed, "I don't know how we made a five on a simple little hole like that!"

"What do you mean?" her husband shot back. "You had three of them."

• • •

474. Two men were about to start a game of golf one day, and just as one was about to tee off, a funeral procession drove by on the road beside the course. The golfer promptly took off his cap, placed it over his heart, and waited for the entire procession to go by. He then put his cap back on and proceeded to tee off.

The other golfer remarked, "Gee, that was a very nice gesture on your part—very thoughtful and respectful."

"Well," explained the first golfer, "it was the least I could do. We were happily married for thirty years."

• • •

475. A guy runs into the clubhouse screaming for someone to call an ambulance. "Someone call an ambulance! I just hit my wife with a tee shot and I think she's dead."

A few minutes go by. An ambulance, fire truck, and several squad cars arrive at the golf course and proceed to the fifth hole. A detective comes over to where the man is standing, near his wife, and starts to question him about what happened.

"Well," says the man, shaking, "I teed up my shot and the ball hit her in the side of the head."

The detective looks over the body and says, "I see an indentation in her temple that says Topflight 3, but what's this mark on her thigh that says Titlest 2?"

"Oh, that was my Mulligan!"

• • •

476. For twenty years four old friends met in Florida every Christmas morning to enjoy a game of golf. Each year their wives made it harder and harder for the foursome to meet.

"This is costing me a new Corvette," complained the first guy.

The second guy topped him with, "Oh yeah? This is costing me a trip to Europe!"

Not to be outdone, the third guy said, "That's nothing. I had to give my wife my American Express card and a plane ticket to New York."

The fourth guy was quiet. "Say, what about you? You're awfully quiet. What did this year's trip cost you?" the others inquired.

The fourth guy just smiled. "It's simple. I woke my wife up at five this morning and said, 'Golf course or intercourse?' She said, 'I'll get your clubs!'"

• • •

477. A foursome had played golf every Saturday morning at the local club for the last ten years. One of the guys was an incredible player. He would play right-handed for a couple of weeks, and then play left-handed for a couple of weeks, both with equal skill. His one annoying trait was that every couple of weeks or so he would be thirty minutes late.

One morning, shortly after this guy had landed his second tee shot just two feet from the pin, one of the others decided to ask him why he golfed right-handed and then left-handed.

"What's up with you? Why do you keep switching sides every couple of weeks?" asked one of the golfers.

"It's like this," said the guy. "Every Saturday morning when I wake up, I turn over and look at my wife. If she's sleeping on her right side, I tee off right-handed. If she's on her left side, I play left-handed."

"What if she's on her back?" persisted the golfer.

"That's when I'm thirty minutes late!"

• • •

478. The classroom was full of pregnant women and their husbands, and the Lamaze class was in full swing. The instructor was teaching the women how to breathe properly and informing the men how to give the necessary assurances at this stage.

The instructor said, "Remember, ladies, exercise is good for you. Walking is especially beneficial. And, guys, it wouldn't hurt you to go walking with your partner!"

The room got really quiet. Finally, a man in the middle of the group raised his hand.

"Question?" said the instructor.

"Is it all right if she carries a golf bag while we walk?"

• • •

479. A man playing as a single at Hilton Head was teamed with a female twosome. After a few holes one of the women asked why he was playing such a beautiful course by himself. He said that he and his wife had played this same course every year for over thirty years, but that she had passed away. He explained that he kept the tee time in her memory.

The first woman said, "Certainly someone would have been willing to take her spot at such a beautiful course."

The man said, "That's what I thought, but they all wanted to go to her funeral."

• • •

480. A woman is cleaning out her attic and comes across a small cigar box. She opens it and finds three golf balls and $350. When her husband comes home she questions him; he breaks down and admits that every time he was unfaithful to her he put a golf ball in the box. She immediately gets mad, but thinks better of it and says, "Forty years of marriage and only three golf balls. This doesn't make me very happy, but I forgive you. I understand the golf balls, but I still don't know what the three hundred and fifty dollars is all about."

"Well," her husband answers nervously, "every time I had collected a boxful of golf balls, I sold them."

• • •

481. A man waiting to tee off at the local public course saw a funeral procession going by and couldn't help but think how strange it all looked. The casket and the pallbearers were led by a man who had a dog on a leash, and the rest of the people were walking single file behind the casket. Unable to restrain his curiosity, he went up to the man with the dog and asked, "Excuse me for being nosy on such a sad occasion, but I have never seen such a strange funeral procession. I mean, what's with the dog and all the people walking in a straight line?"

The man with the dog said, "This is my wife's funeral."

"But why the dog?" asked the golfer.

"She died because this dog bit her," said the man with the dog.

"I'm very sorry to hear that. Um, would it be possible to borrow the dog for a day or two?"

"Sure," said the man with the dog, "but you'll have to wait in line!"

• • •

482. A couple whose passion had waned in recent years decided to see a marriage counselor. It seemed to help a bit at first but turned bad after that. The counselor, not knowing how else to help the two, grabbed the man's wife and kissed her passionately for a minute.

"There," he said to the husband. "Did you see that? That's what she needs. Good loving every Monday, Wednesday, Saturday, and Sunday."

"Just a minute, fella," retorted the husband. "I can bring her in on Mondays and Wednesdays but Saturdays and Sundays are my golf days."

• • •

483. A wife and her husband were enjoying a quiet evening by the fireplace when the woman inquired, "If I died today, would you remarry?"

"I'm a young man, so probably," said the man.

"Would you let her live in this house?" she asked.

"Well, houses are expensive these days—probably so," he replied.

"Would she cook in my kitchen, sleep in our bed, use our bath, and drive my car?" she continued.

"Well, I suppose she would," he said.

"And would she use my golf clubs?"

"Absolutely not!"

"If she'd use everything else, why not?"

"She's left-handed!"

• • •

484. A woman called her best friend in tears, moaning that her husband had left her. "Don't get so upset," counseled the friend. "That scoundrel has left you countless times before, and every time he comes begging you to take him back."

"This time it's different," sobbed the woman. "This time he took his golf clubs."

• • •

485. One member of a regular Saturday foursome was having an unusually bad day on the links. "Say, what's eating you today? Your game is all over the place," said one of the golfers.

"Aw, it's my wife. Seems all we do is argue all the time. We can't agree on anything," said the first golfer despondently.

"Have you thought about getting professional help?" asked the second.

"Oh, sure, but I can't decide whom I should see, a marriage counselor or my golf pro."

• • •

486. A guy walks into the clubhouse, orders three shots and a beer, drinks them all at once, and starts crying hysterically. Another golfer walks over and says, "Hey, pal. It can't be all that bad. What's wrong?"

"My wife just left me for my golfing partner," he cries.

"It's okay. Calm down. There are plenty of other women out there," says the other golfer.

"I don't care about her," he sobs. "But he's the only guy I could ever beat!"

• • •

487. Every morning for the last three months a golfer was out on the links playing eighteen holes. The club pro noticed this and asked the fellow, "Say, how is it that you can get away every day to play golf? Doesn't your wife care?"

"I went to the doctor's office for my annual physical," said the golfer. "He said I was in good shape but needed to get more iron every day. I told my wife I was doing this under doctor's orders."

Just then the club pro saw a woman running toward the golfer with a big skillet in her hand. "Well, don't look now, but you're about to get some more!"

• • •

488. An avid golfer fought with his wife for years about the amount of time and money he spent away from home on golf. One day, he died suddenly while on the back nine at his club. At the funeral home the director asked what the widow would like in his obituary, to which she replied:

My husband liked to play the game
But now he's in a heap.
My revenge for him never being home:
"Ping clubs for sale—and cheap!"

• • •

489. Two women meet for their weekly round of golf one Wednesday morning. One has a new bag and new clubs.

"Say, nice set of clubs you have there," says the first woman.

"Yeah, they're from my husband," explains the second. "I caught him fondling the maid and he bought me these."

"You fired the maid, didn't you?" asks the first.

"Are you kidding? I'm holding out for new shoes and a cart!"

• • •

490. A husband and wife were playing golf one Wednesday morning. On the thirteenth green the wife collapsed from a heart attack.

"Get some help! Hurry!" she said.

The husband reassured her and ran off to find a doctor. A little while later he returned, walking rather slowly. He picked up his putter and began to line up his shot.

His wife raised up her head and said, "What the hell are you doing? I may be dying and you're putting!"

"Not to worry," said the husband. "I found a doctor on the fourth hole who said he would come and help."

"The fourth hole?" she replied. "How soon before he gets here?"

"Hey, I said don't worry," said the husband. "He was putting out on four and everyone ahead of him agreed to let him play through."

• • •

491. A grillroom manager walked over to a golfer who had been drinking for six hours after playing a round of golf. Worried about serving drinks to someone who was obviously inebriated, the manager said, "Sorry, bud, but I can't serve you any more drinks today."

The golfer, somewhat blurred, looked up at the manager and said, "I'll have you know I just lost my wife, pal!"

"I'm sorry to hear that, sir. It must be very hard losing a wife," commented the manager.

"Hard?" said the golfer. "It was damn near impossible!"

• • •

GOLFING AND WOMEN

492. A golfer walked into the clubhouse shortly after he had begun playing a round with three women. He had several bruises and a 7-iron wrapped around his neck.

"What happened to you?" asked the club pro.

"Well, I was playing with that threesome of women you put me with. One of them hooked a tee shot into the cow pasture next to the first fairway. She was having trouble

locating her ball, so I climbed over the fence to look in the pasture. Just when we were about to give up, I noticed that a cow had a golf ball stuck under its tail. Trying to be helpful, I lifted the cow's tail and asked her, 'Hey, lady, does this look like yours?'"

• • •

493. Two men were having a very slow round of golf because the two ladies in front of them seemed to get caught into every sand trap, lake, and rough on the course. They never motioned for the men to play through. Finally, after taking two hours to play four holes, one of the men said, "I think I'll walk up there and ask those women to let us play through." He walked out on the fifth fairway, got halfway to the women, stopped, turned around, and came back.

"Well, what did they say?" asked the second man.

"I can't do it. One of those women is my wife and the other is my mistress! Maybe you should go talk to them."

The second man walked toward the women, got halfway there, and hurried back.

"What's the matter?" asked the first man.

"Small world, isn't it?"

• • •

494. A young couple met at Augusta and fell in love. On the last night of their vacations they were discussing how they would continue the relationship.

"I think it's only fair to warn you that I'm an avid golfer," said the man. "I live for the sport."

"Well, since you're being so honest, so will I," she said. "I'm a hooker."

"I see," he said. He thought for a moment and added, "It's probably because you're not keeping your wrists straight when you hit the ball."

• • •

495. Q: Why does it take a woman with PMS twelve strokes to get to the green on a par-4 hole?
A: IT JUST DOES, OKAY!

• • •

496. A business owner got a frantic phone call at the office one day from his wife asking him to buy some barbecue supplies she had forgotten to buy earlier. He said he'd be happy to go to the store, but only *after* his golf league that night. So, after playing golf he stopped at the store and picked up three bags full of supplies. He walked out of the store to his new Cadilac. Because the grocery bags were so full and so heavy, he wasn't able to reach into his pants pocket to pull out his keys to open the trunk. He saw a beautiful woman walking nearby and asked her, "Could you please do a favor for me?"

"Um, sure," she said.

"These bags are heavy and I can't seem to reach into my pants pocket to get my keys to unlock the trunk," he explained. "Do you think you could grab the keys and unlock it for me?"

"No problem," she said, smiling.

When she reached in for the keys, two golf tees came out with them. She bent over, picked them up, and asked, "What in the world are these things for?"

"Oh, those are to keep my balls in the air while I'm driving."

"Wow," she remarked, "those Cadillac people think of everything!"

• • •

497. One sunny Saturday afternoon a golfer is getting ready to tee up on the first hole. Out of nowhere a young lady in a full wedding gown comes running toward the golfer, crying and screaming the whole time. "I can't believe this! How could you do this on our wedding day?" she sobs.

The golfer calmly takes his swing and says, "Hey, I said *only* if it wasn't a nice day!"

• • •

498. Two lady golfers met for a round of golf one day. Just as they were getting set to tee off, one said, "Shall we play by the men's rules, or will every shot count?"

• • •

499. The local club pro had to appear before the judge for not paying a few parking tickets. While waiting for his turn, he noticed the judge occasionally glaring in his direction. Finally, the judge called his case. "You look familiar. Where do I know you from?" demanded the judge.

"Oh, I'm the guy that gave your wife all those golf lessons that lowered her score," said the pro, hoping to get a break.

"That's it!" exclaimed the judge angrily. "I'm giving you thirty years of hard labor!"

• • •

500. A local golf pro was trying to drum up business for his club by putting a display at one of the busier shopping malls. He had rented an indoor golf machine so he could give lessons. As he was finishing giving a lesson to a young golfer he noticed two women approaching, one of whom had taken a lesson the day before. "Hello," said the pro. "Would you two ladies like a few free golf lessons?"

"Not me," said the first woman. "I brought my friend to learn today. You taught me how to play yesterday."

• • •

501. Two guys were playing behind a rather slow foursome of ladies one day. They consistently lost balls, flubbed tee shots, and hit into the rough. After the foursome took numerous shots getting to the green and putting out, the first guy heard one say she got a five on the hole. "You know, I think I understand why women play golf," he said.

"Oh yeah? Why is that?" asked the other guy.

"It gives them something to lie about other than their age!"

• • •

This book is heartily endorsed by the author's son, Jordan, future golf champion of the world!

"Accept no substitute!"
Jordan Dohanyos